WEDDING MUSIC FOR VIOLIN AND VIOLA

by Scott Staidle

VIOLA

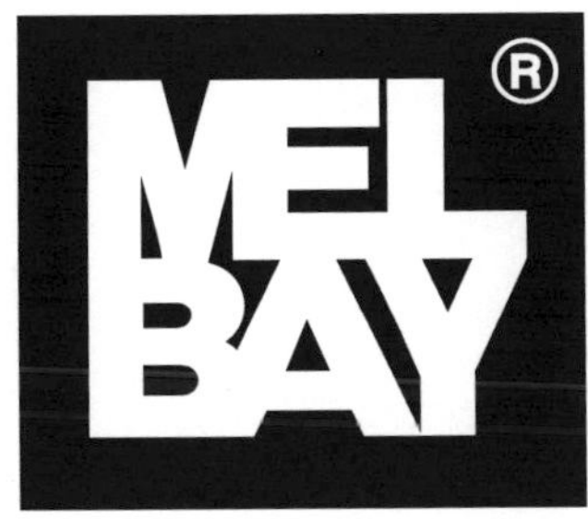

WWW.MELBAY.COM

Contents

Air in "D"
for Violin and Viola

Viola

J. S. Bach
Arr. Scott Staidle

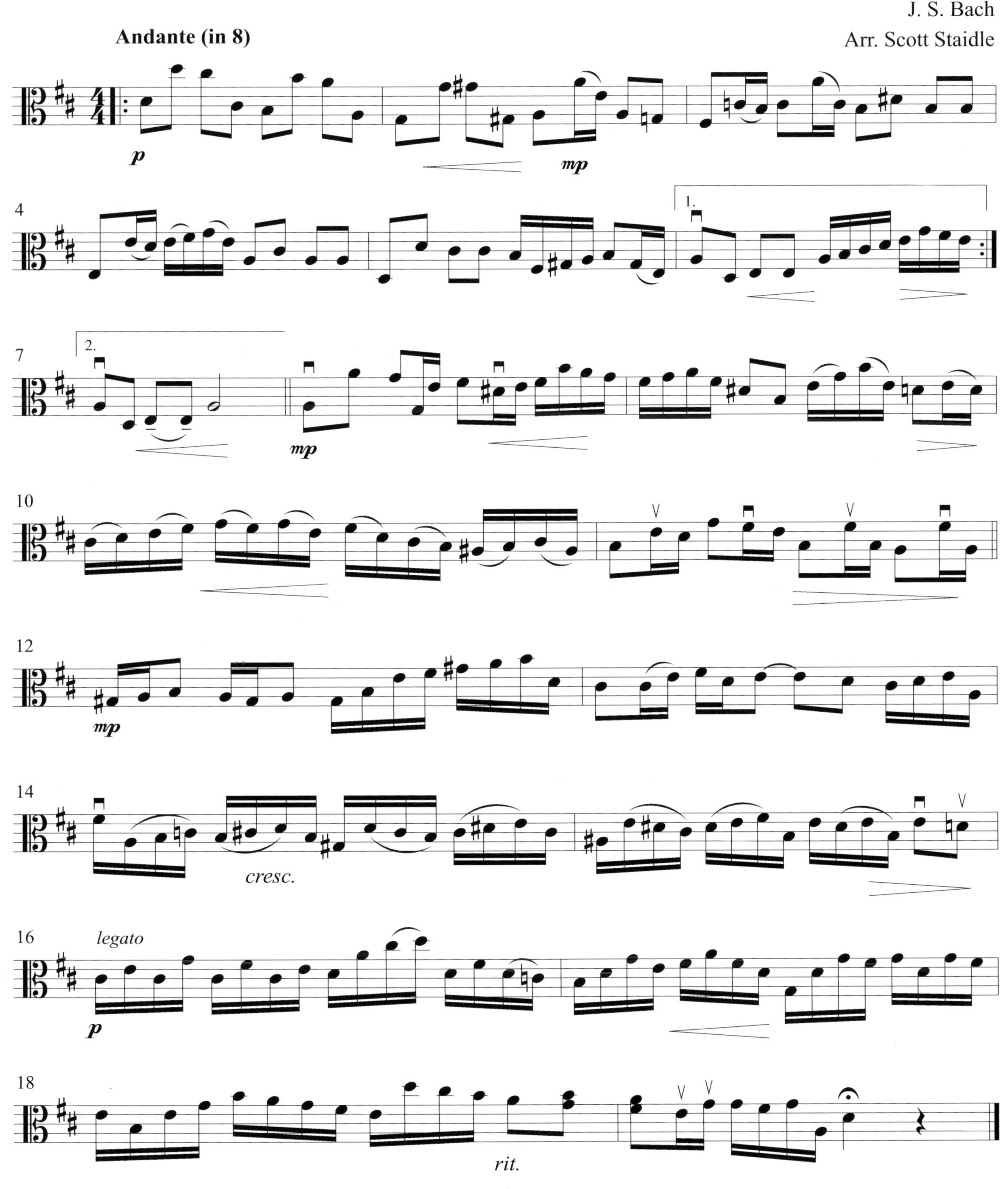

Allegro
for Violin and Viola

Viola

J. H. Fiocco
Arr. Scott Staidle

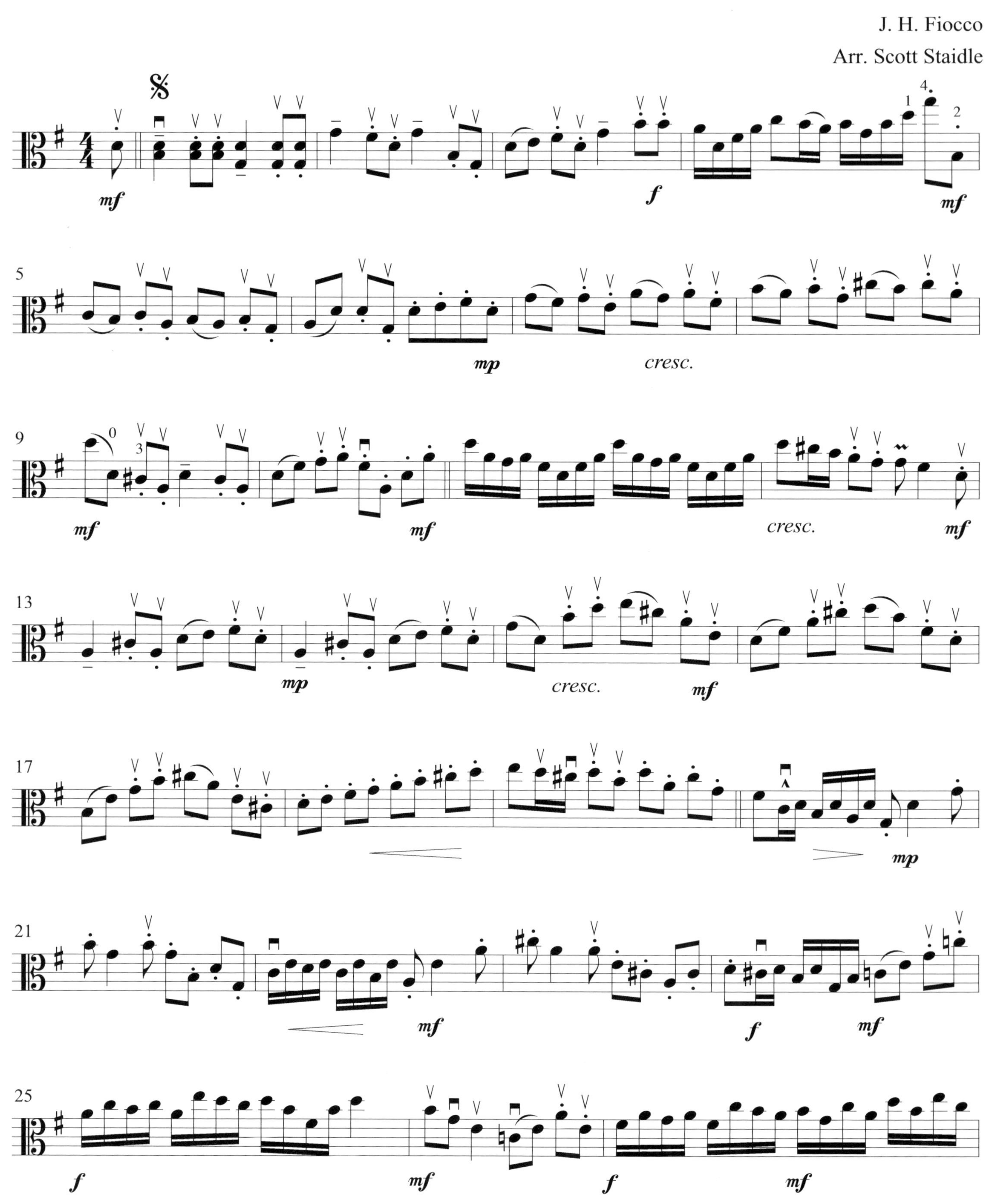

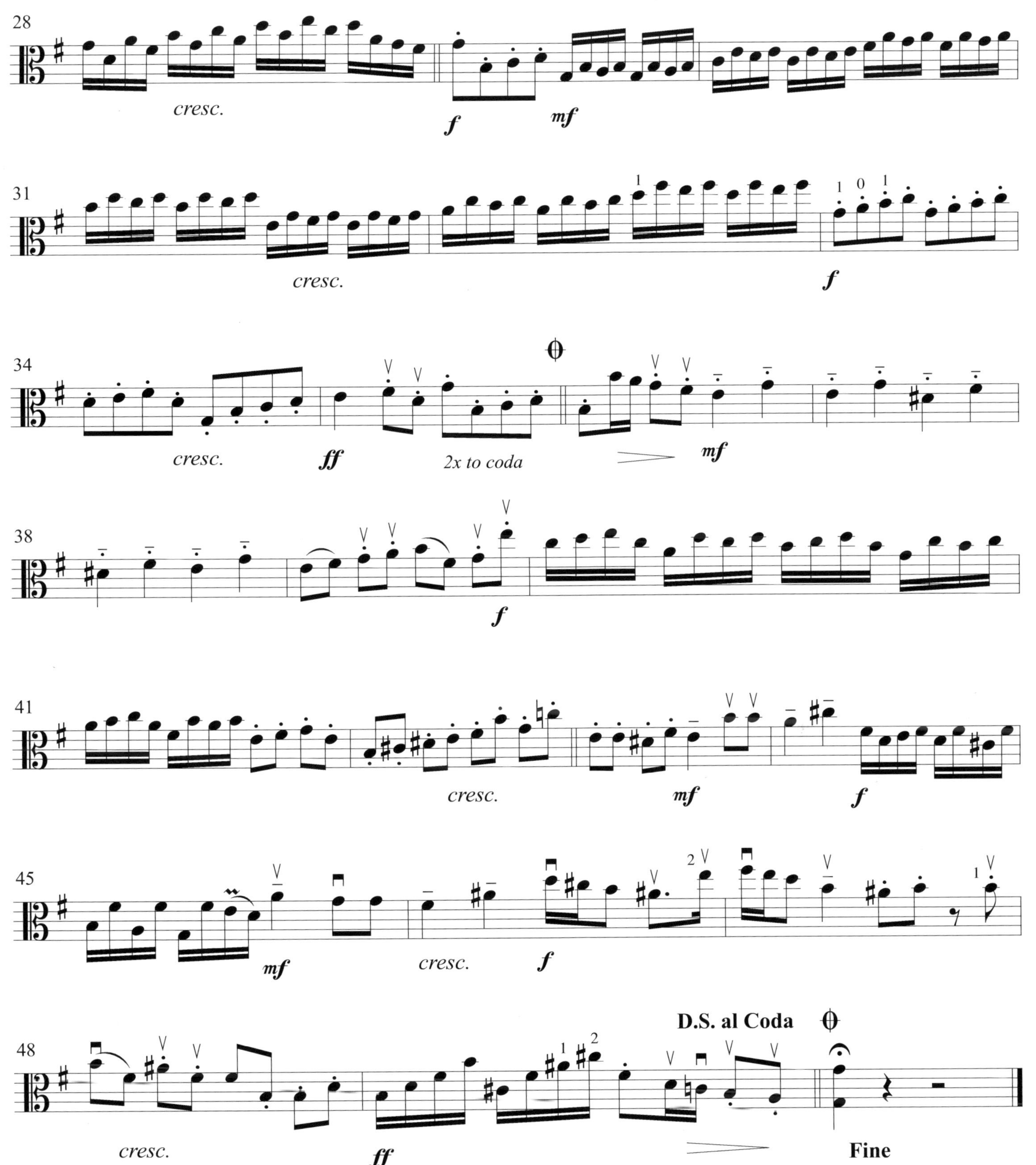
28
cresc.
f
mf
31
cresc.
f
34
cresc.
ff
2x to coda
mf
38
f
41
cresc.
mf
f
45
mf
cresc.
f
D.S. al Coda
48
cresc.
ff
Fine

Amazing Grace
for Violin and Viola

Viola

Traditional
Arr. Scott Staidle

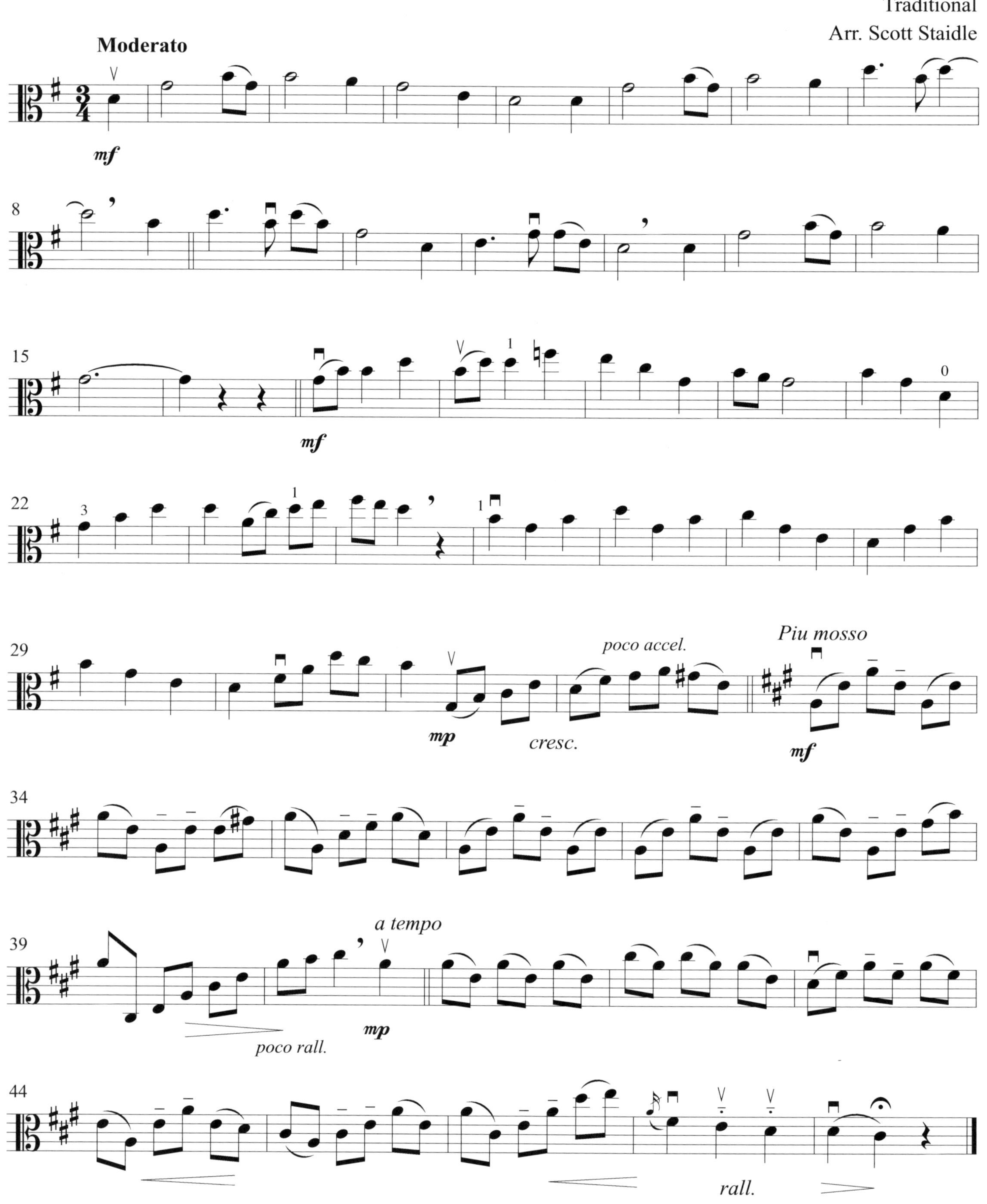

Jesu, Joy of Man's Desiring
for Violin and Viola

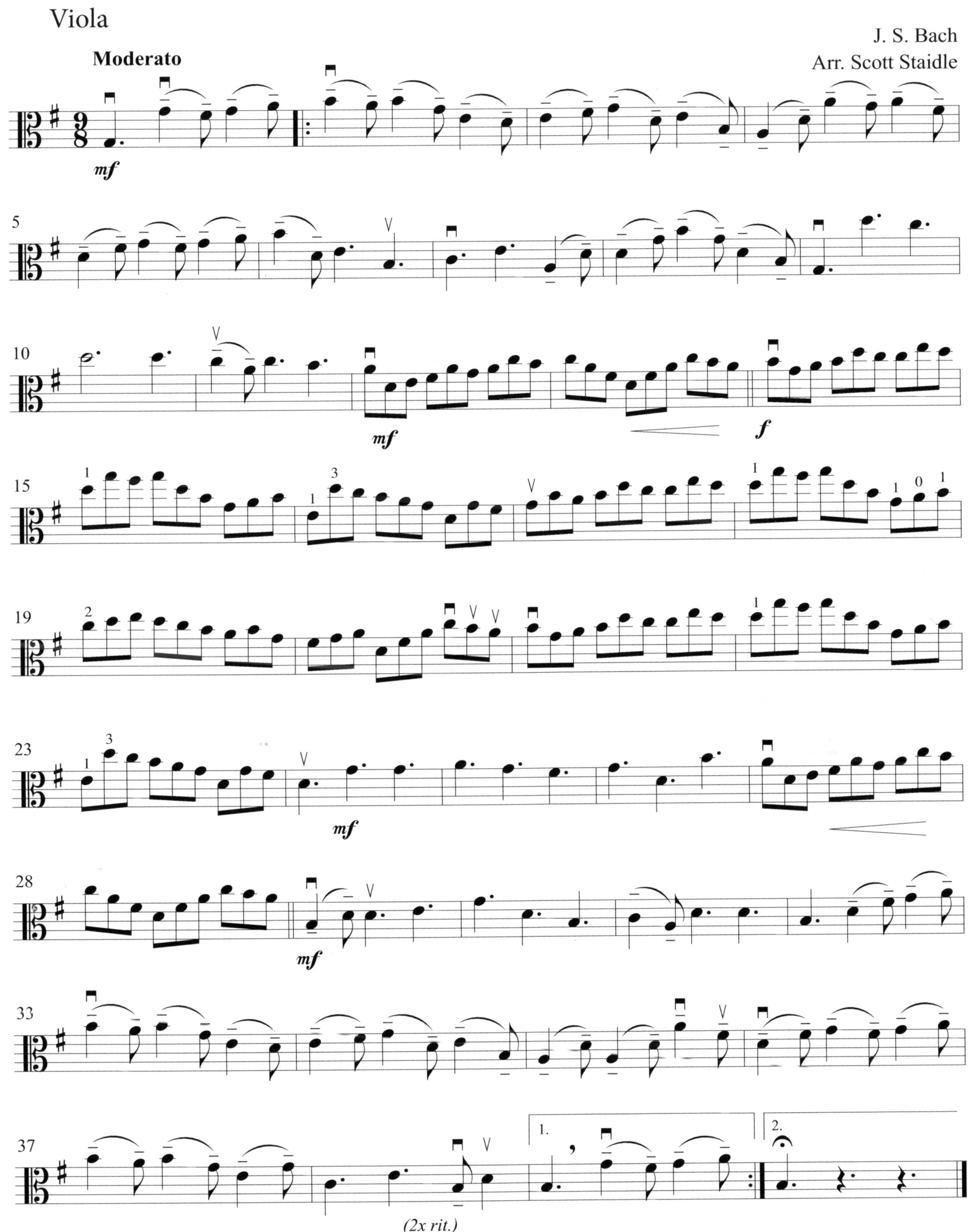

Kanon
for Violin and Viola

Viola

J. Pachelbel
Arr. Scott Staidle

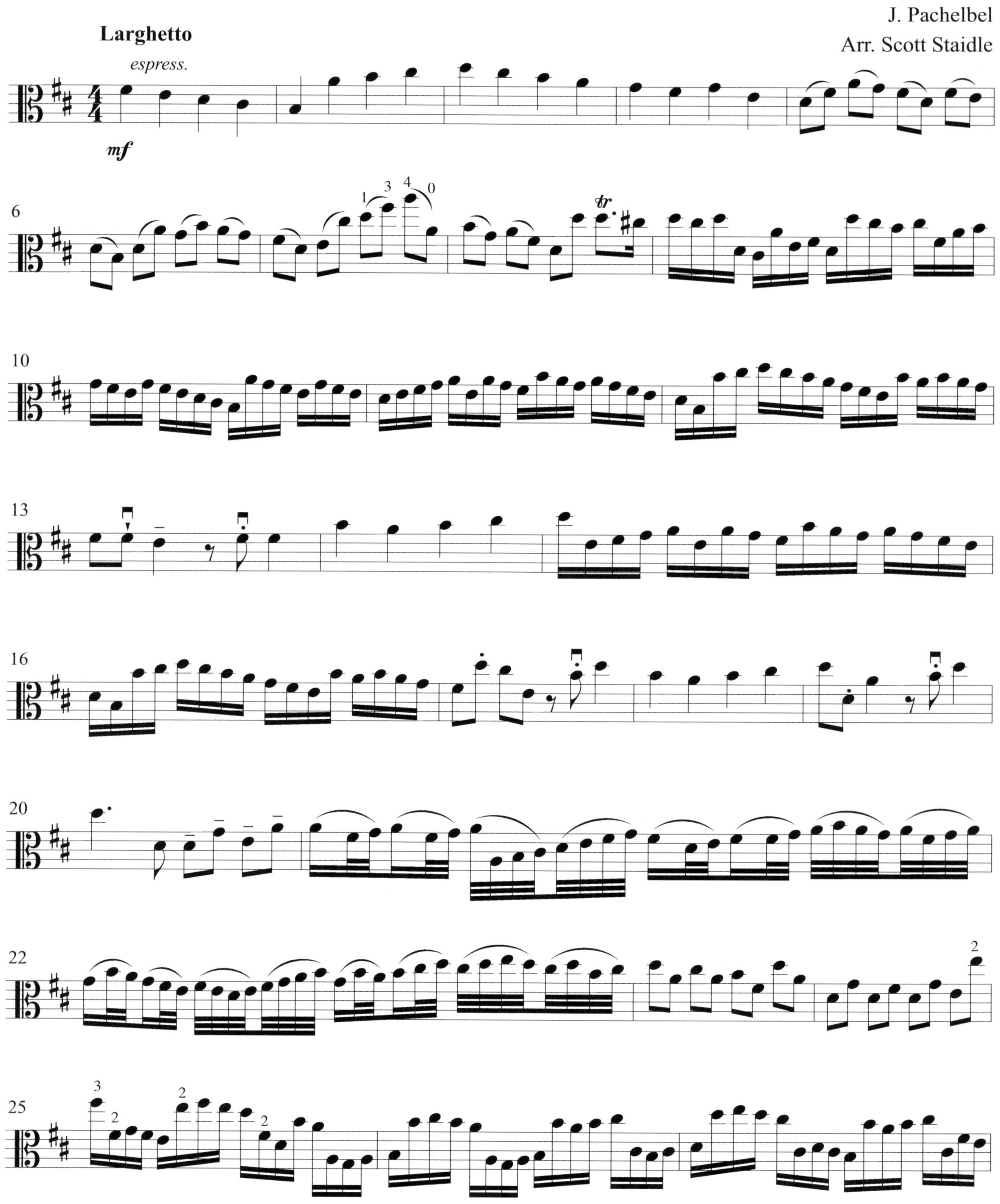

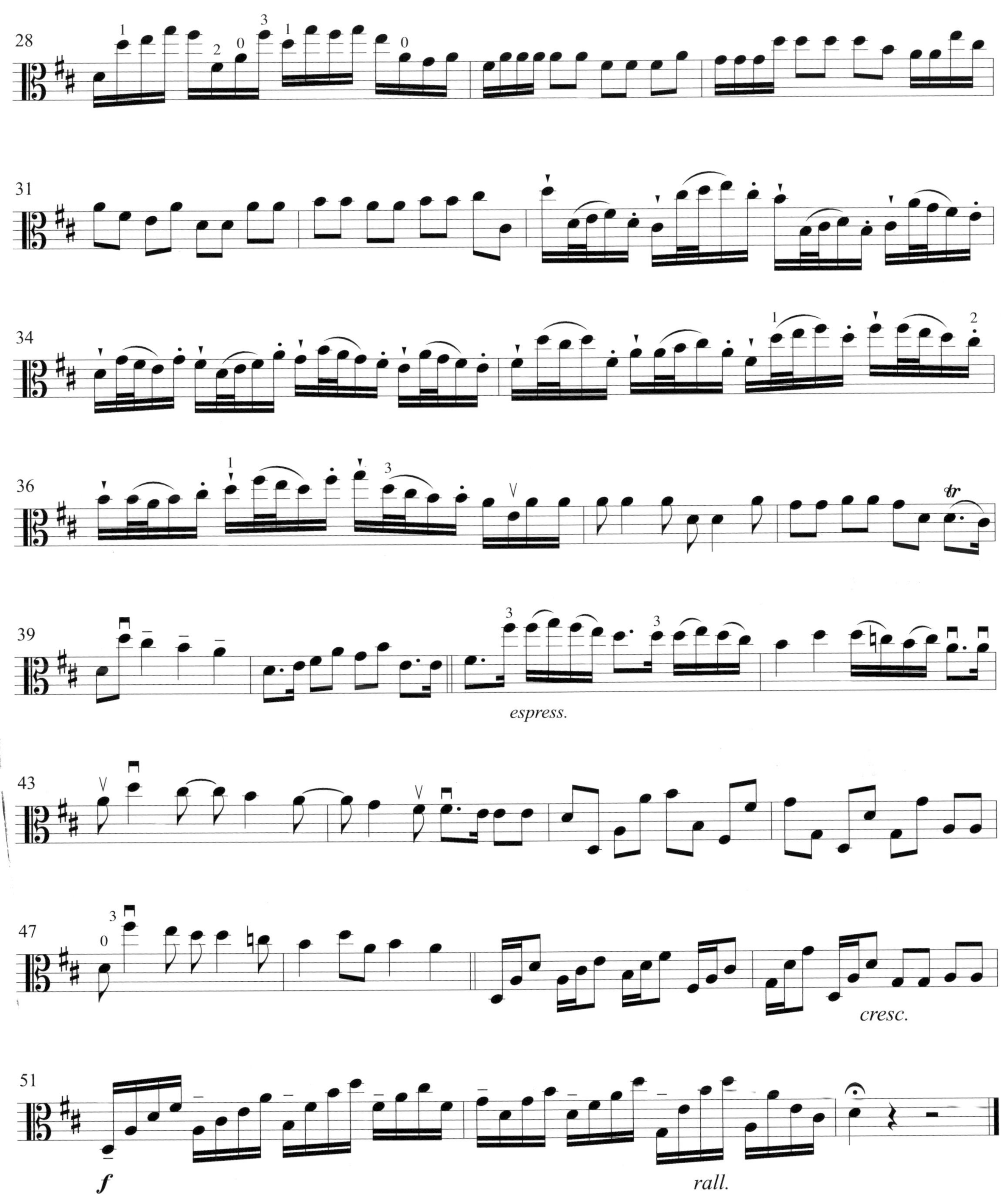

espress.
cresc.
f
rall.

Bridal Chorus
for Violin and Viola

Viola

R. Wagner
Arr. Scott Staidle

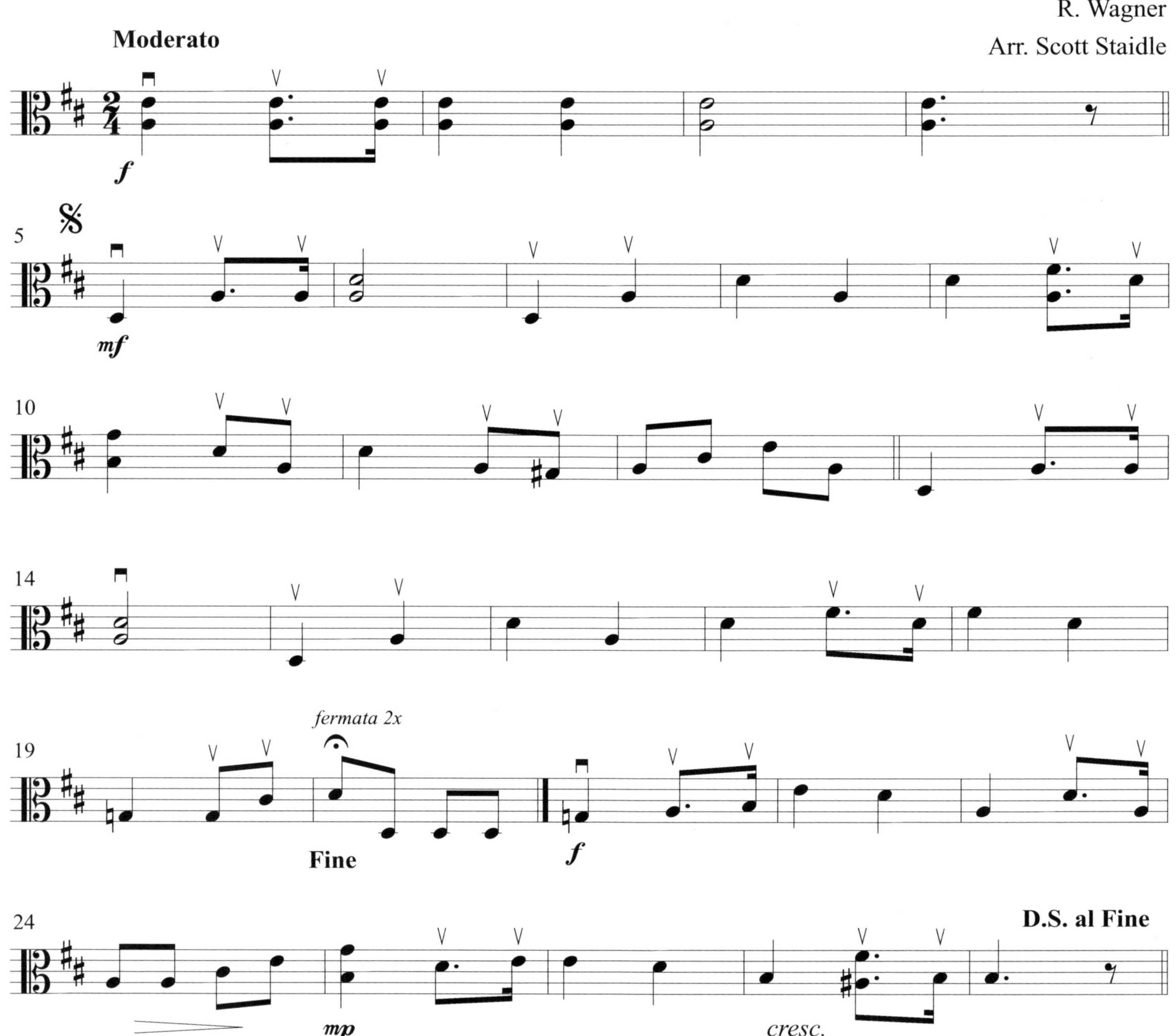

This page is left blank to avoid an awkward page turn.

Menuetto
for Violin and Viola

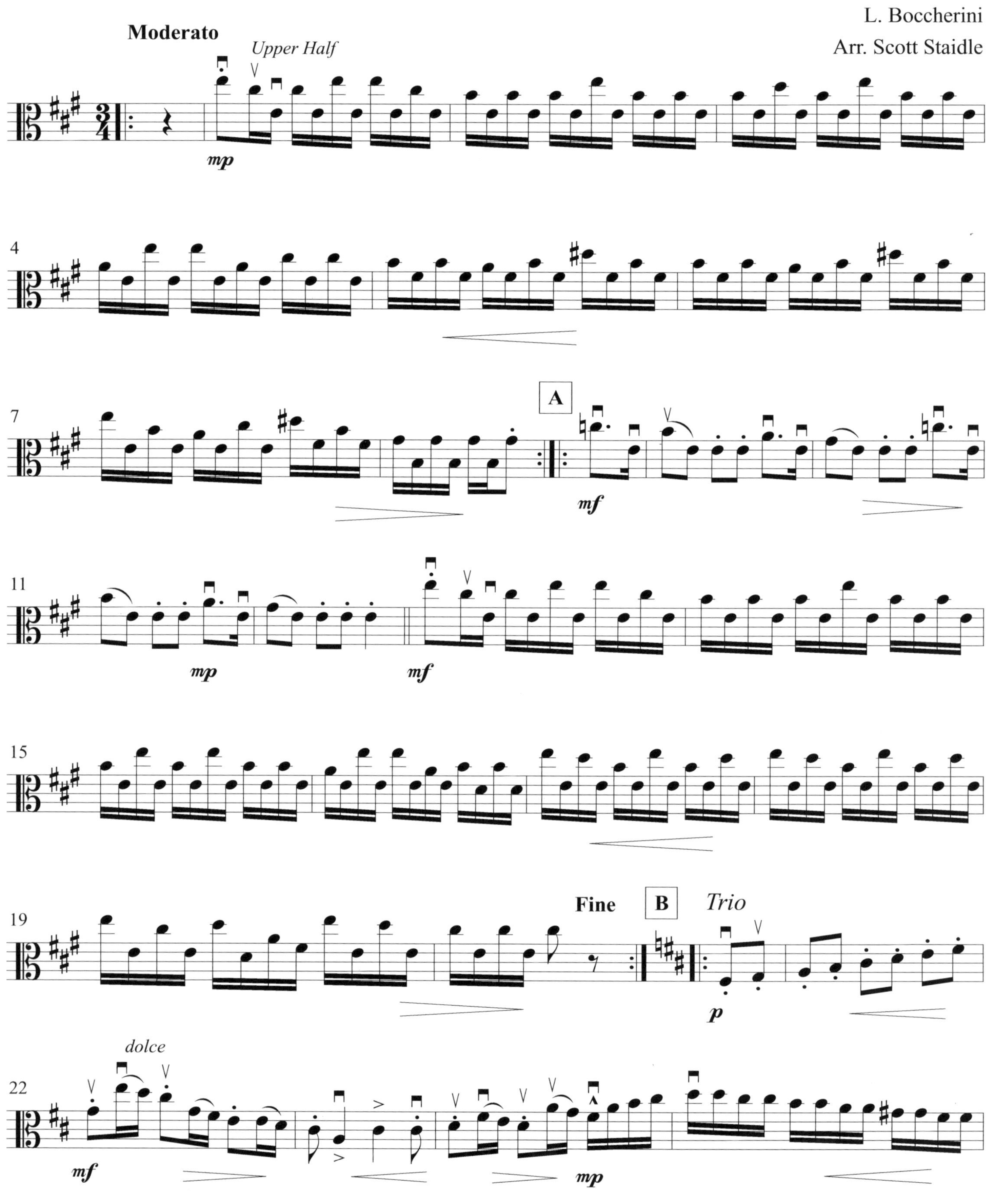

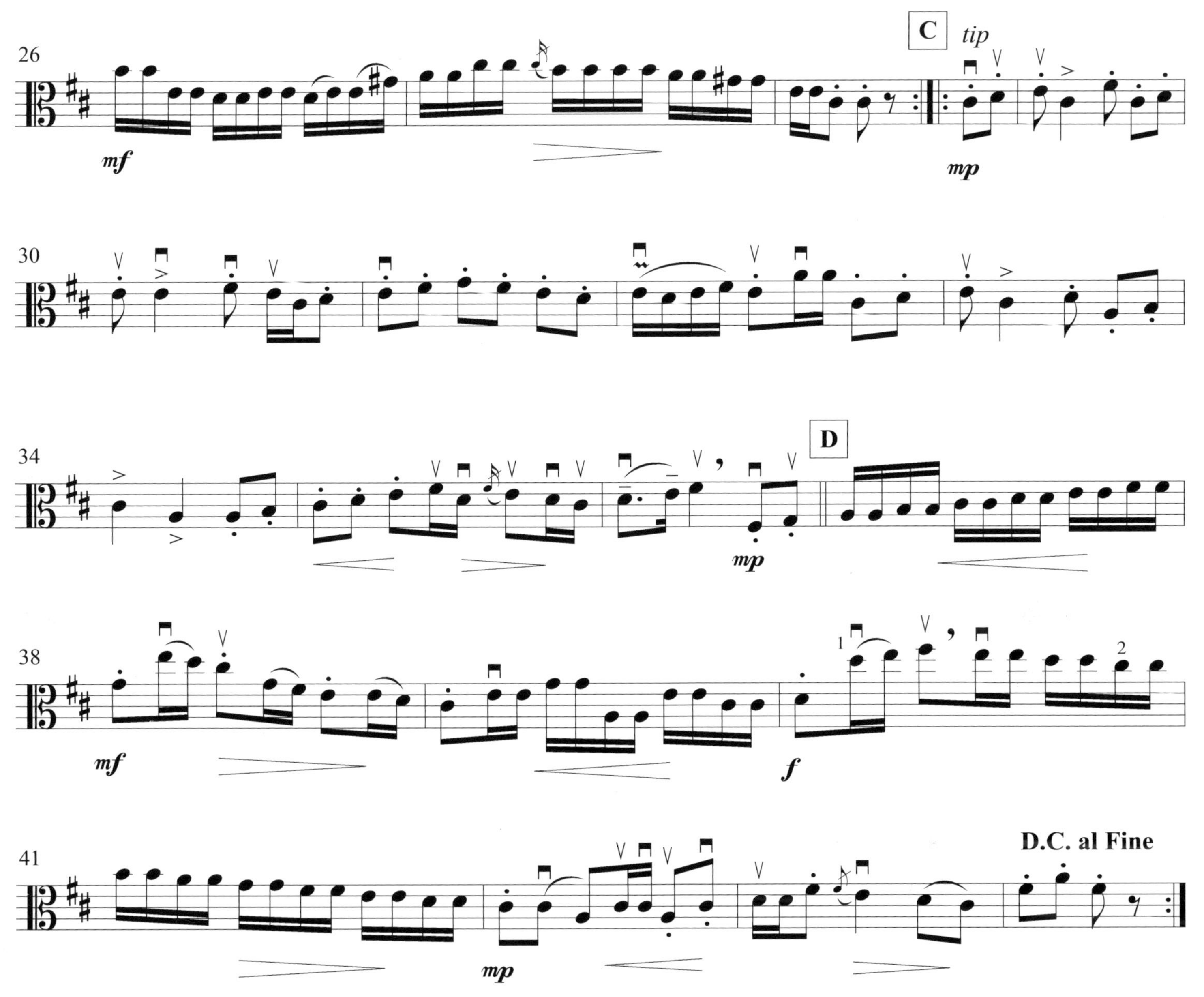
26
C
tip
mf
mp
30
34
D
mp
38
mf
f
41
mp
D.C. al Fine

Ode to Joy
for Violin and Viola

Viola

L. van Beethoven
Arr. Scott Staidle

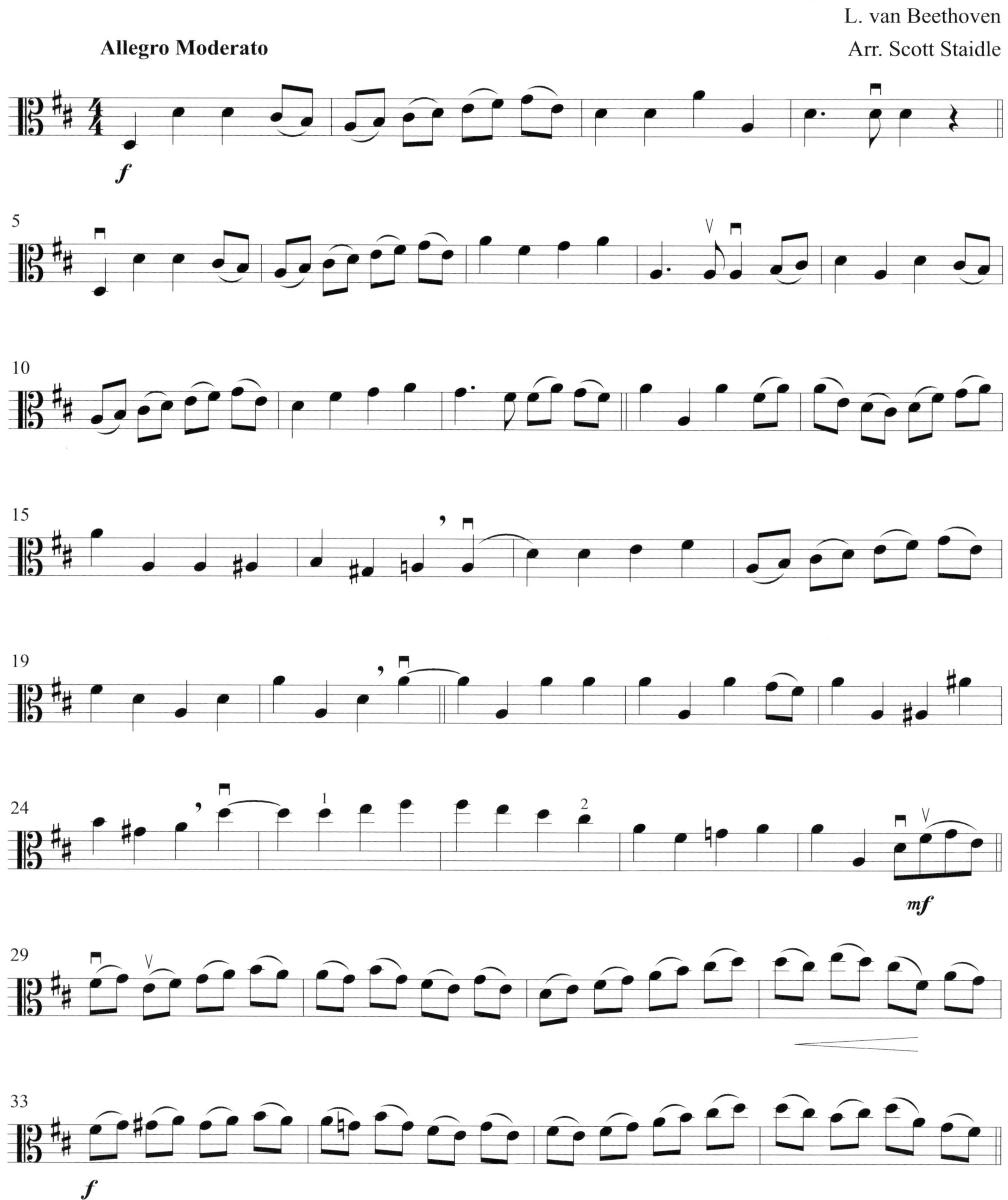

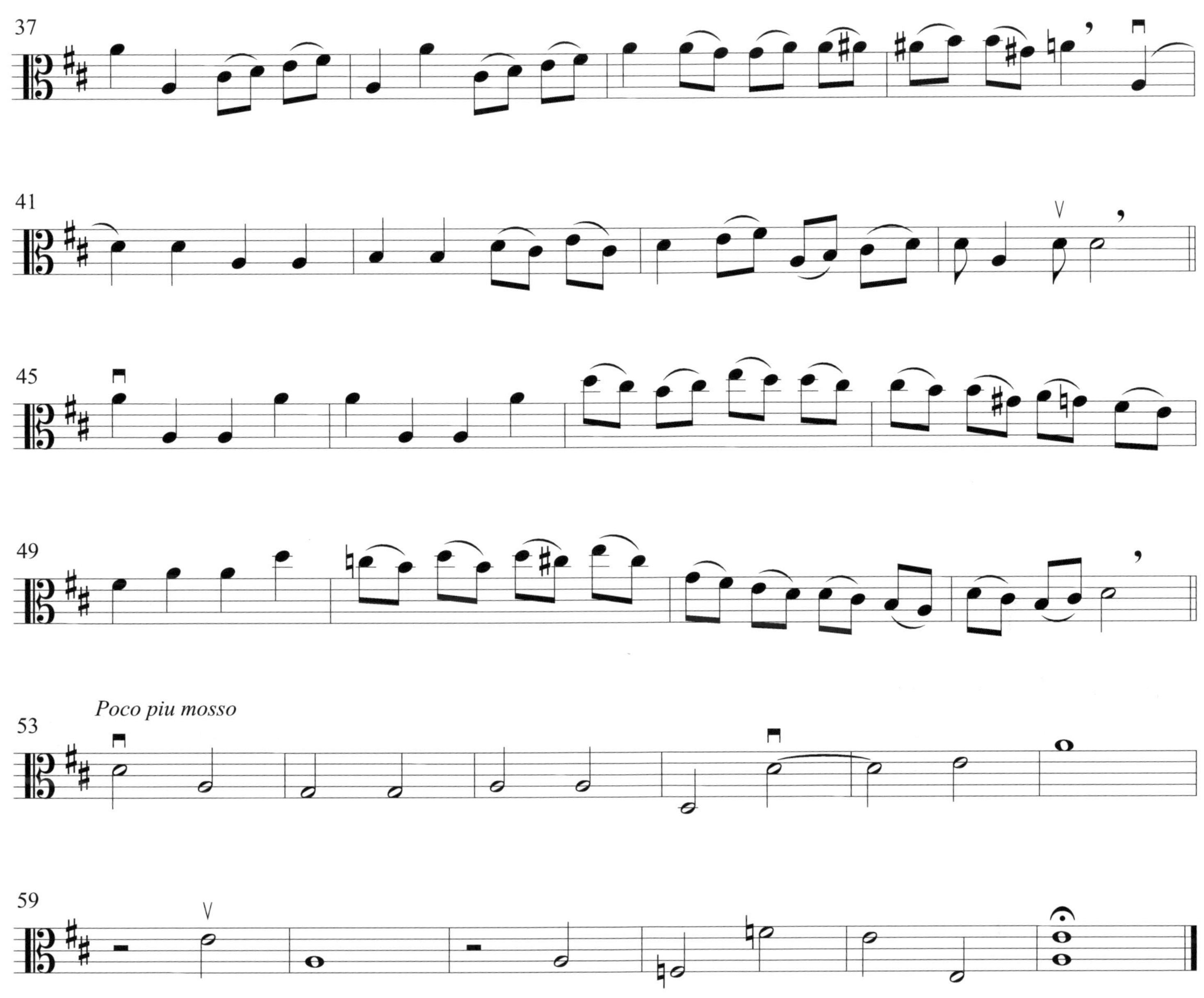
37
41
45
49
Poco piu mosso
53
59

Trumpet Voluntary in "D"
for Violin and Viola

Viola

H. Purcell
Arr. Scott Staidle

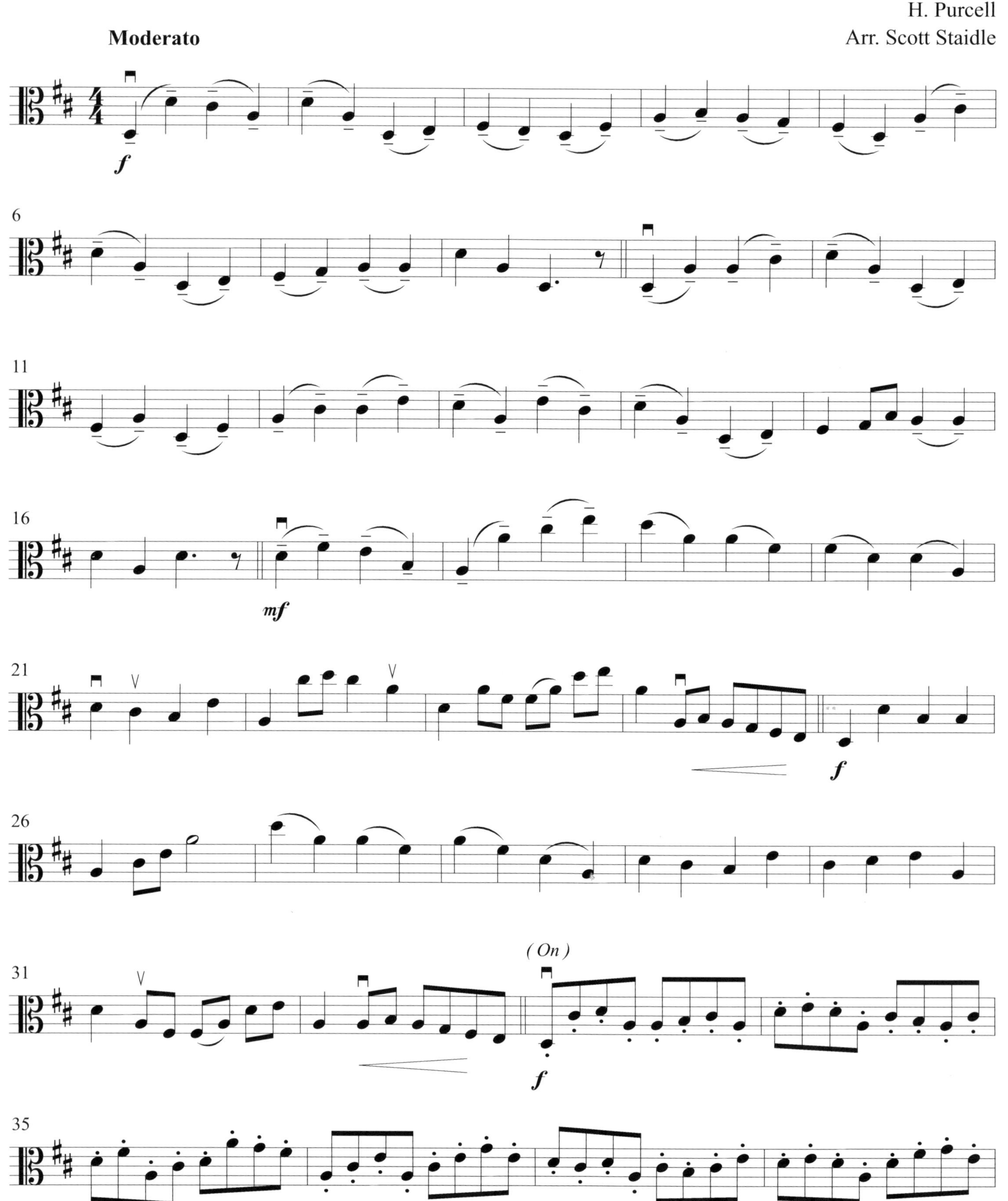

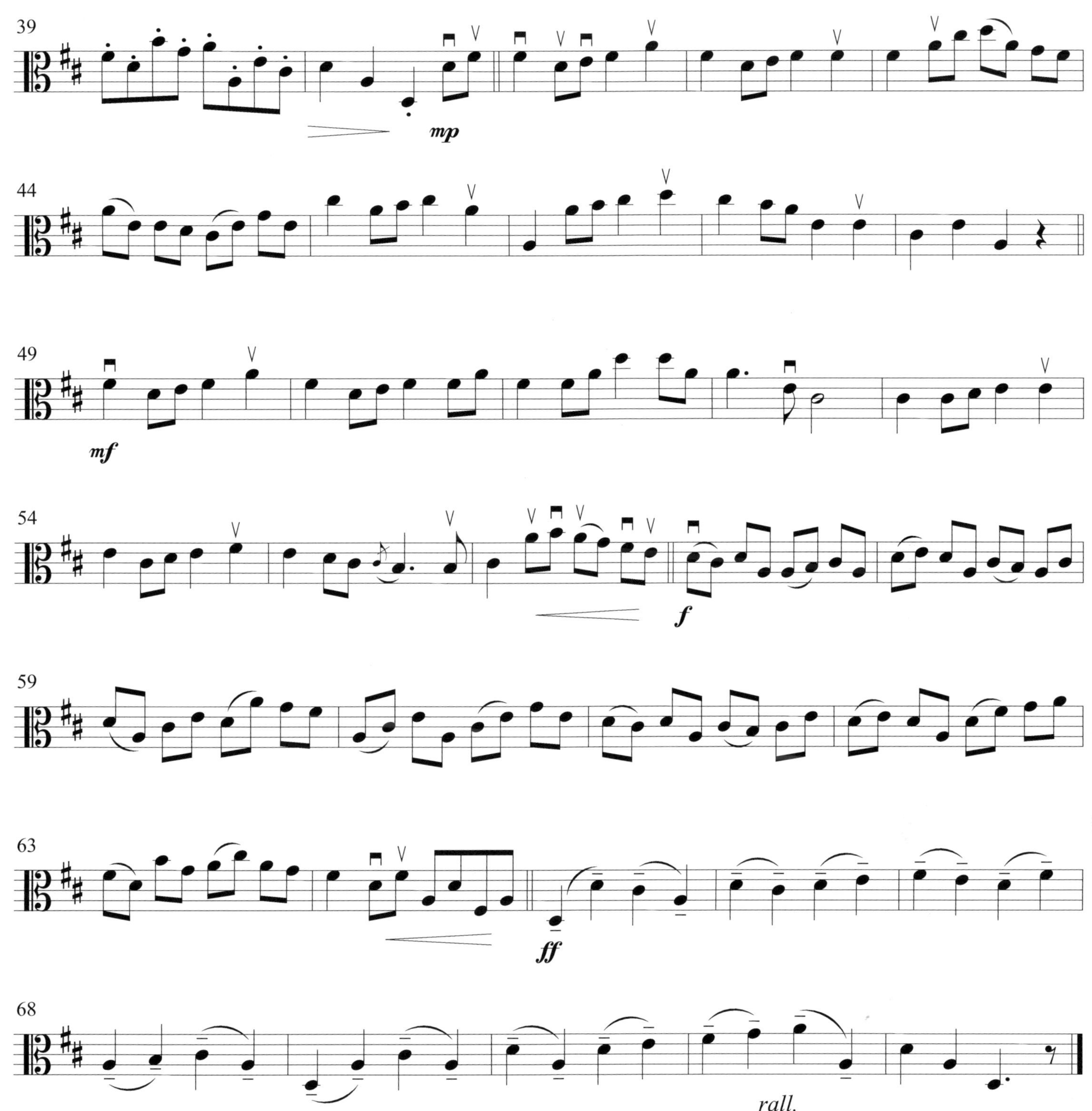
39
mp
44
49
mf
54
f
59
63
ff
68
rall.

Wedding March
for Violin and Viola

Viola

F. Mendelssohn
Arr. Scott Staidle

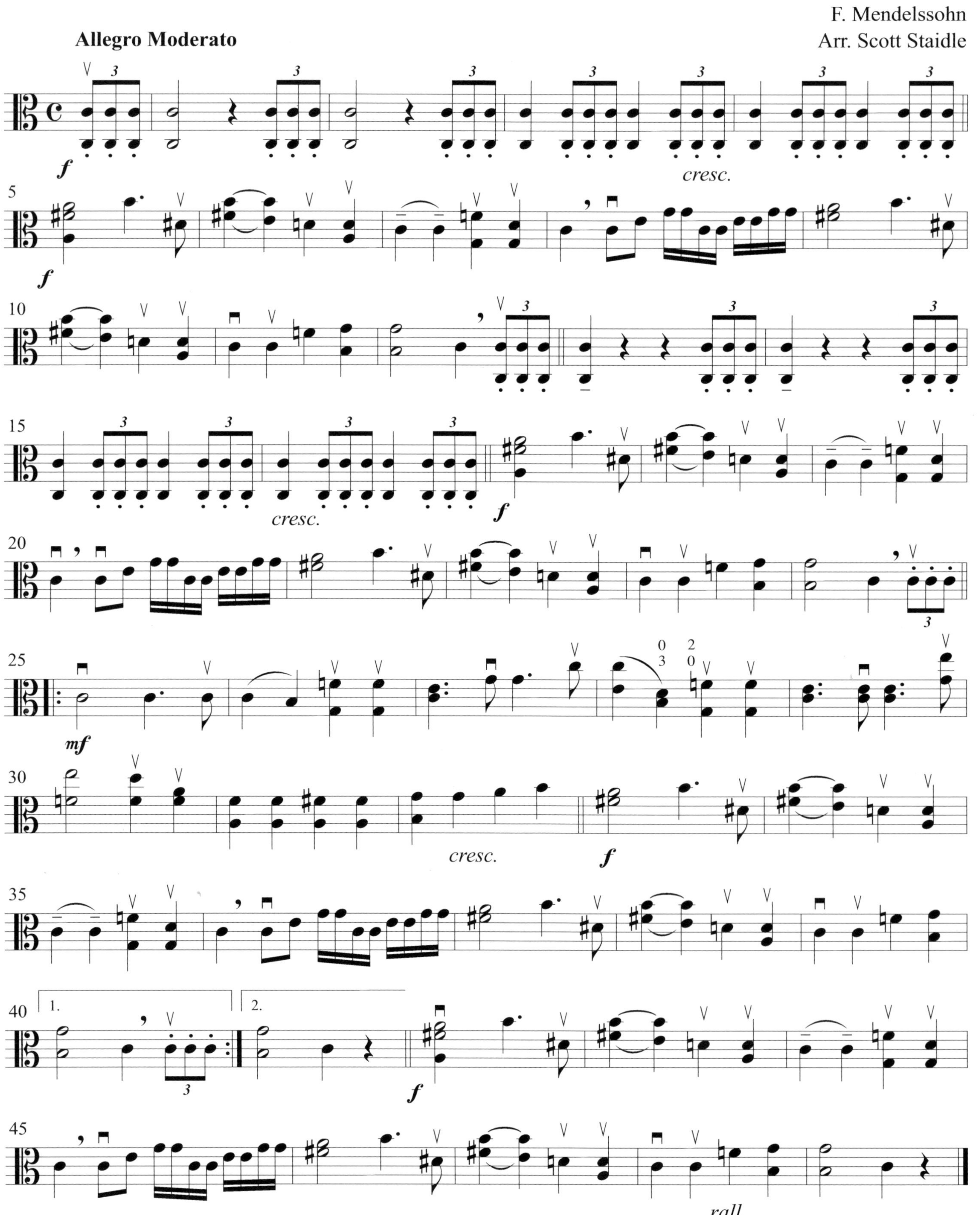

This page is left blank to avoid an awkward page turn.

Rondeau
for Violin and Viola

Viola

J. Mouret
Arr. Scott Staidle

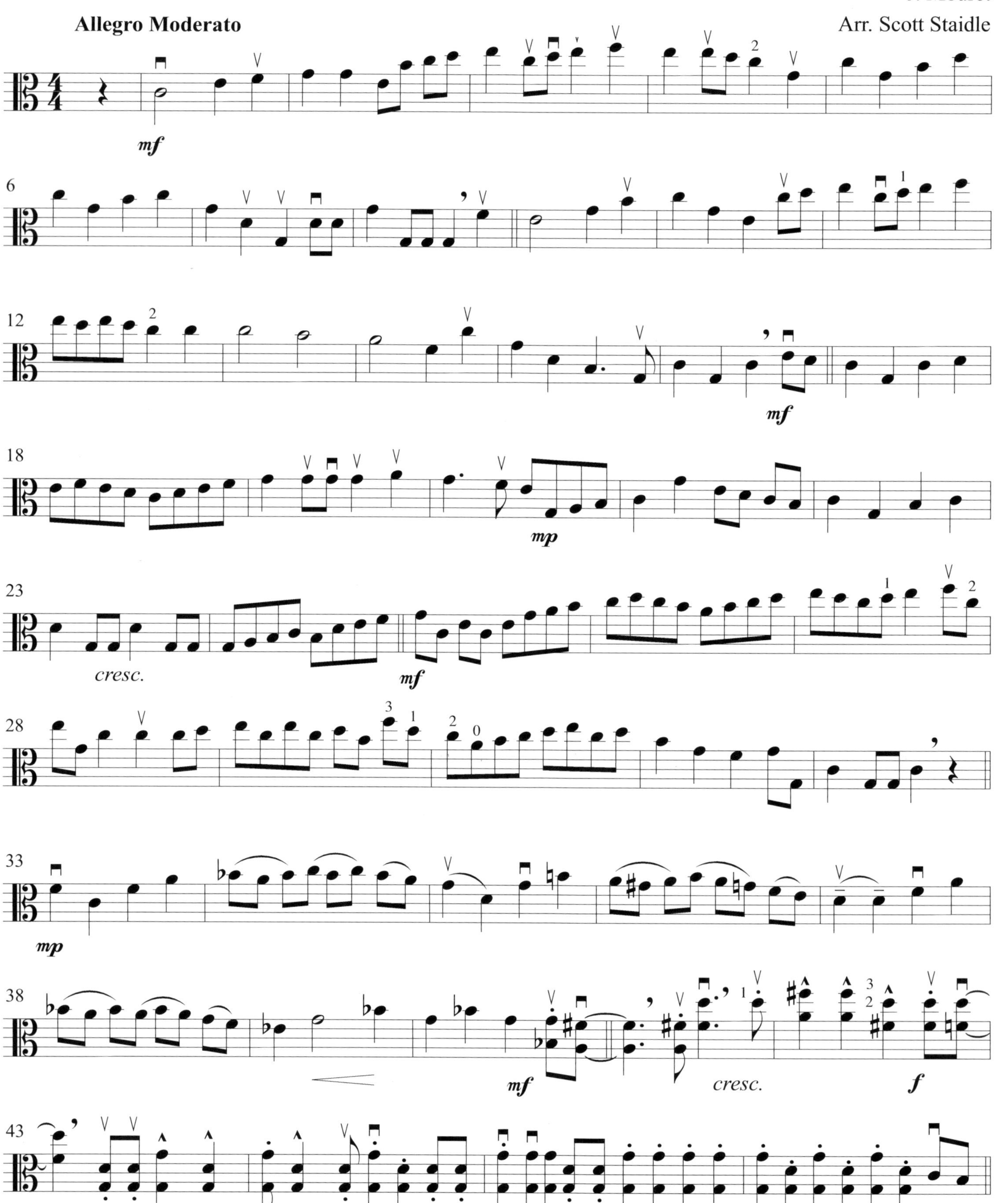

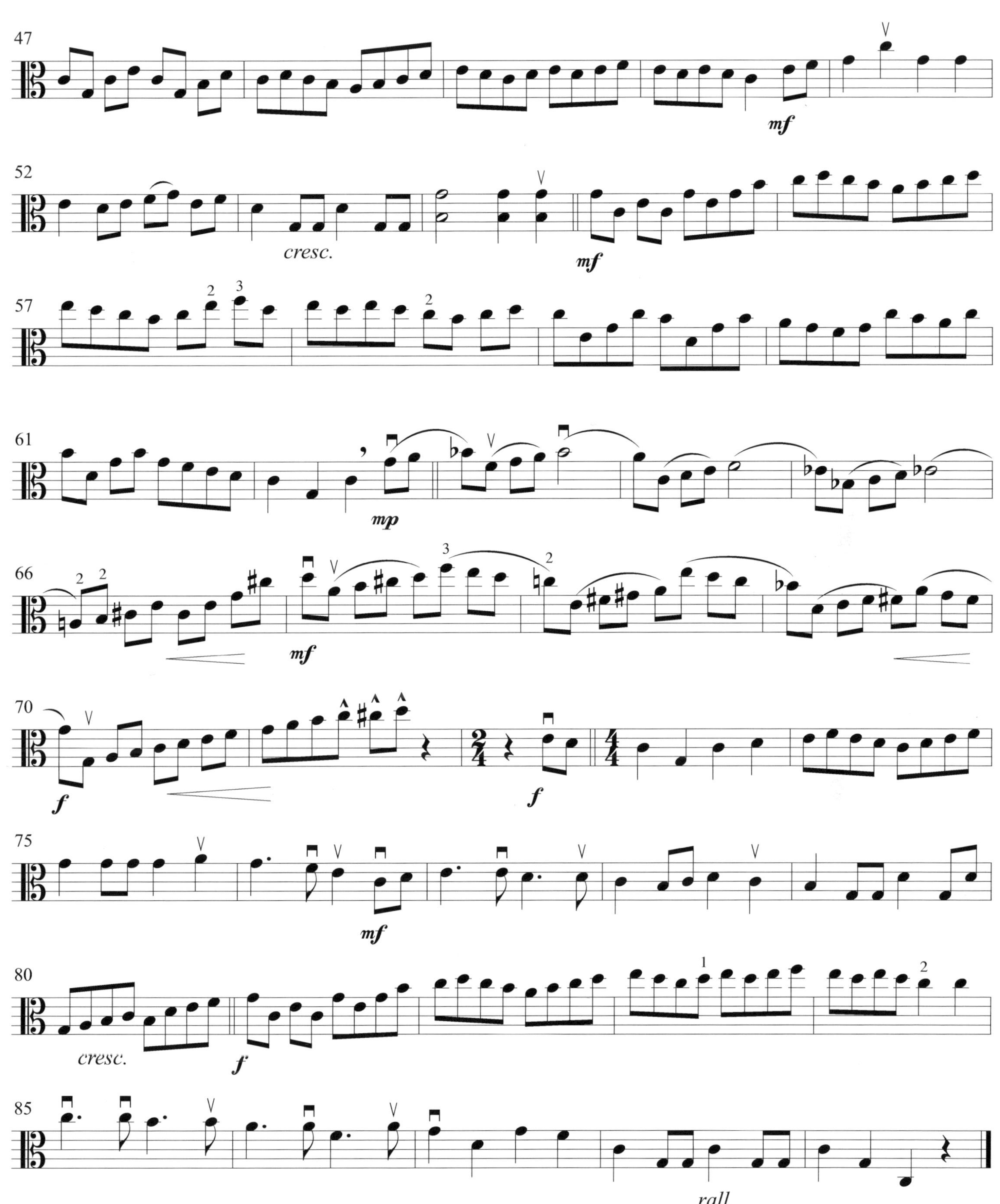
47
mf
52
cresc.
mf
57
61
mp
66
mf
70
f
f
75
mf
80
cresc.
f
85
rall.

Serenade
for Violin and Viola

Viola

J. Haydn
Arr. Scott Staidle

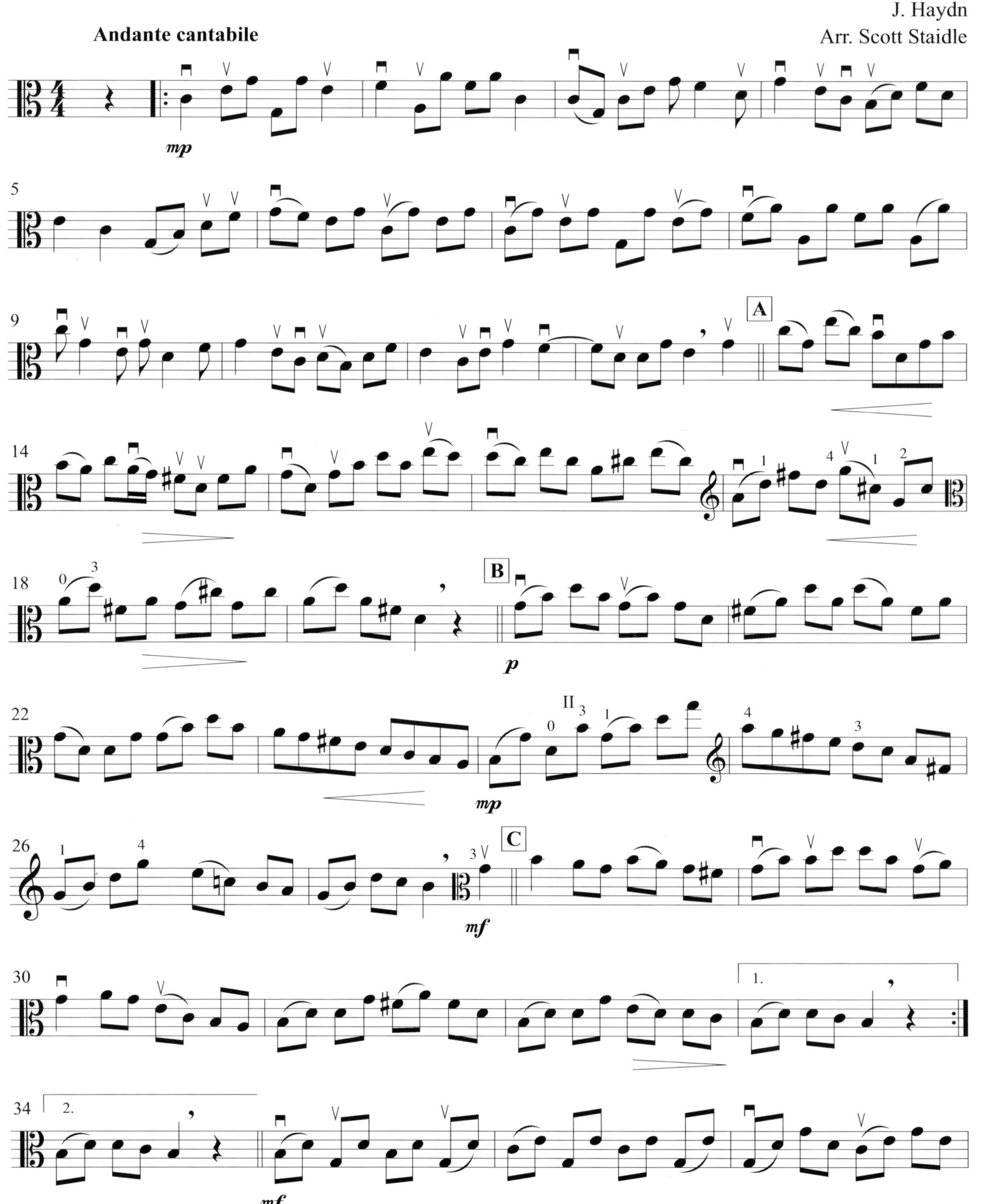

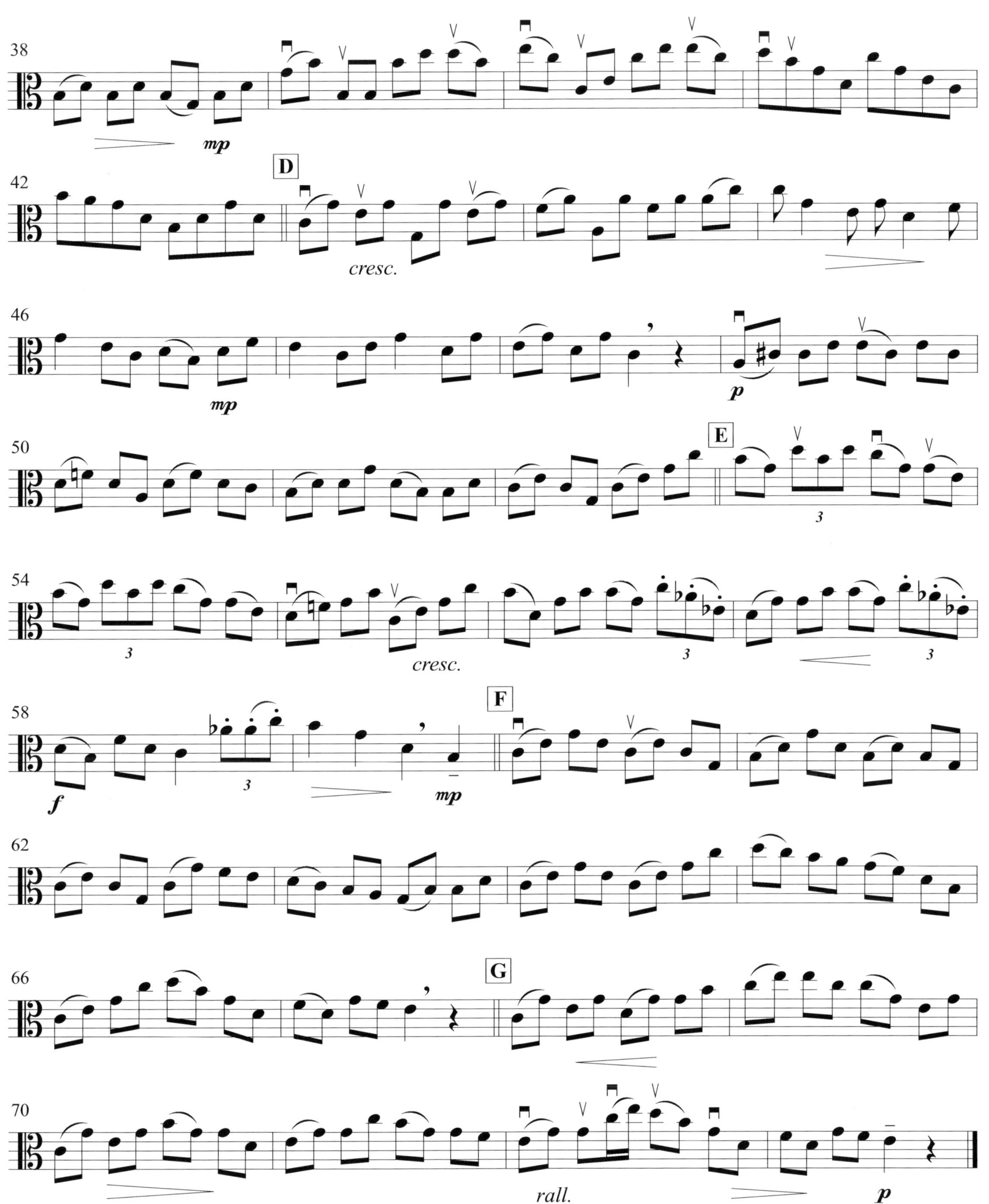
38
mp
42
D
cresc.
46
mp
p
50
E
54
cresc.
58
f
F
mp
62
66
G
70
rall.
p

Water Music - Hornpipe
for Violin and Viola

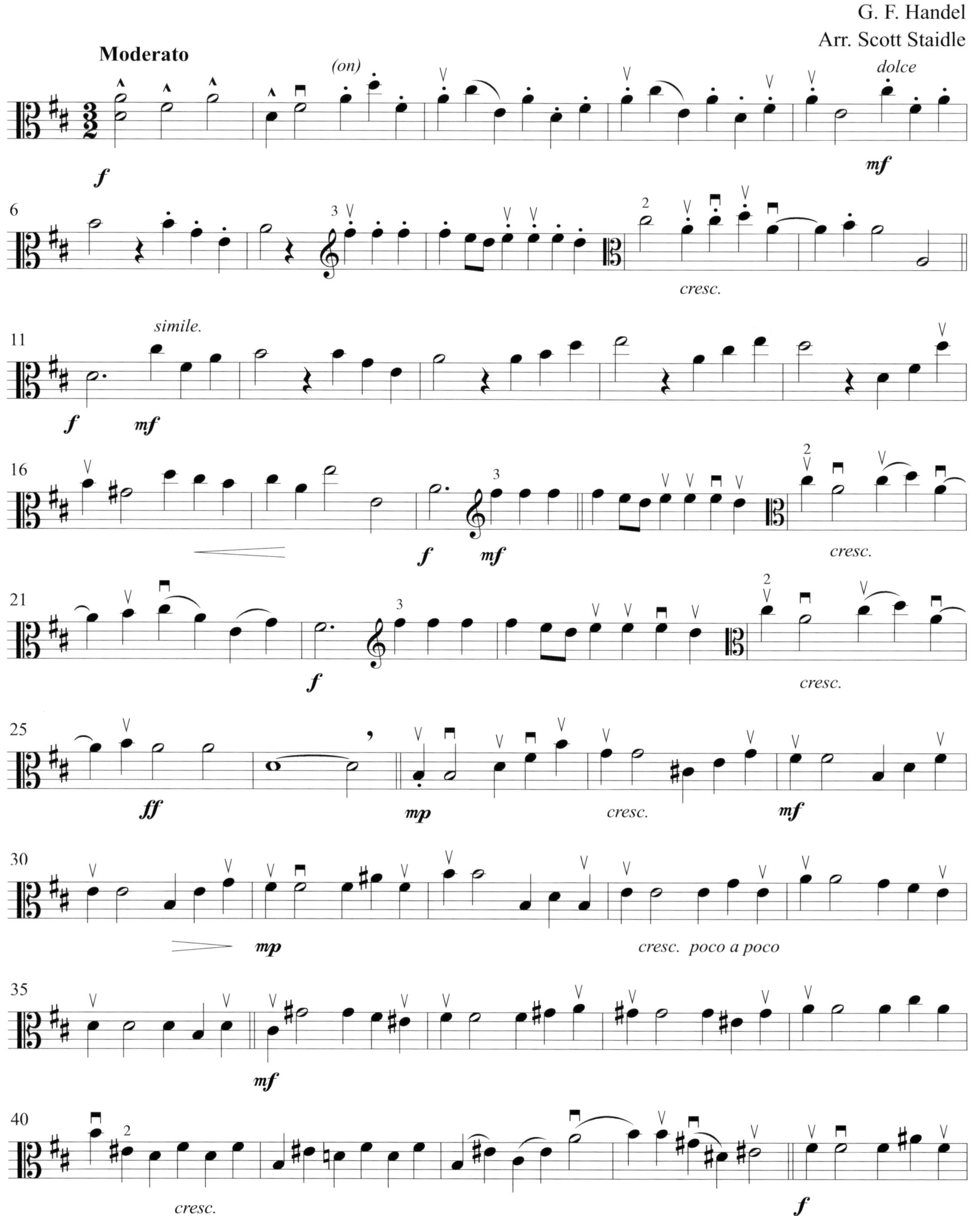

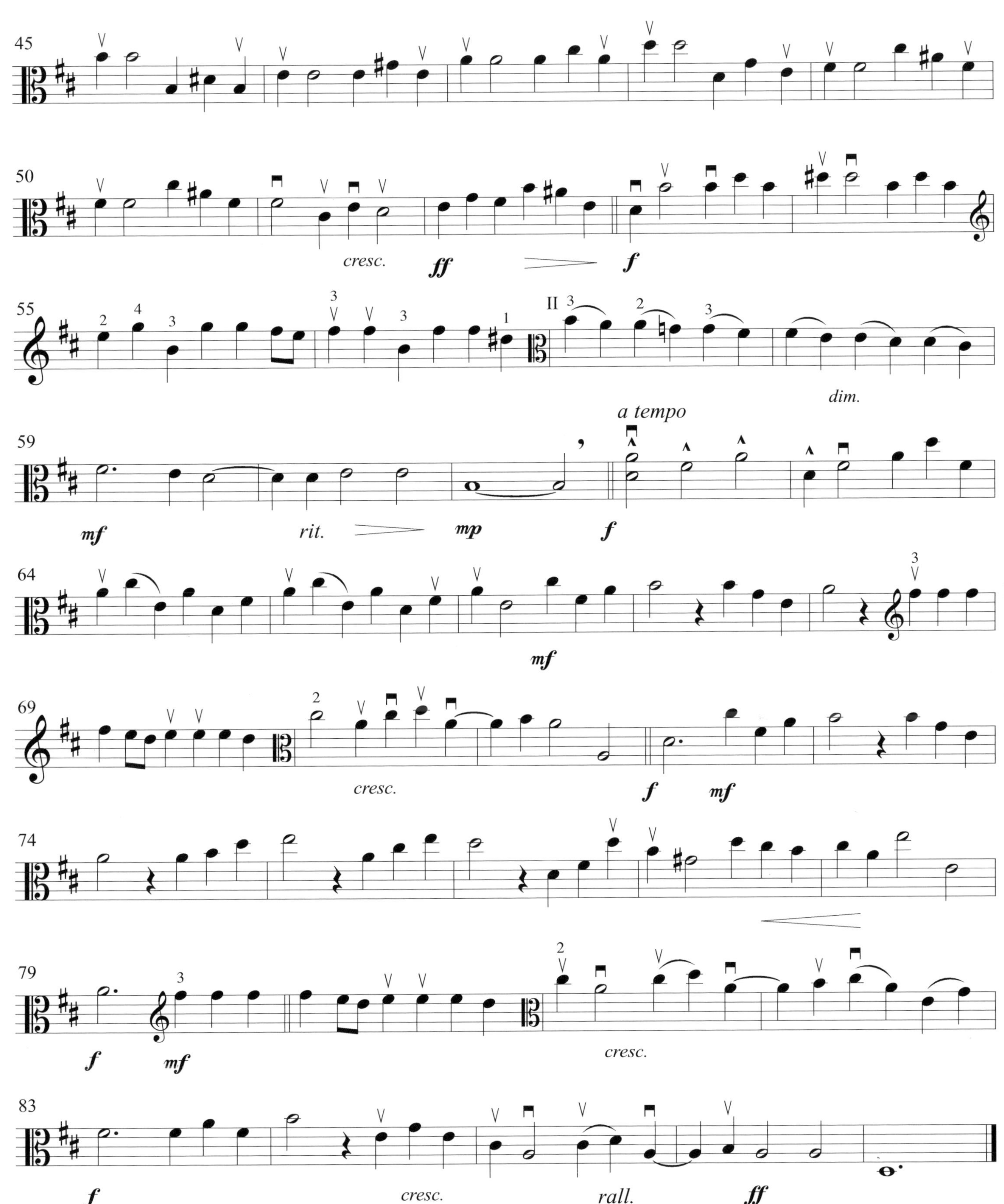
45
50
cresc.
ff
f
55
II
a tempo
dim.
59
mf
rit.
mp
f
64
mf
69
cresc.
f
mf
74
79
f
mf
cresc.
83
f
cresc.
rall.
ff

Winter - 2nd Movement from "The Four Seasons"
for Violin and Viola

Viola

A. Vivaldi
Arr. Scott Staidle

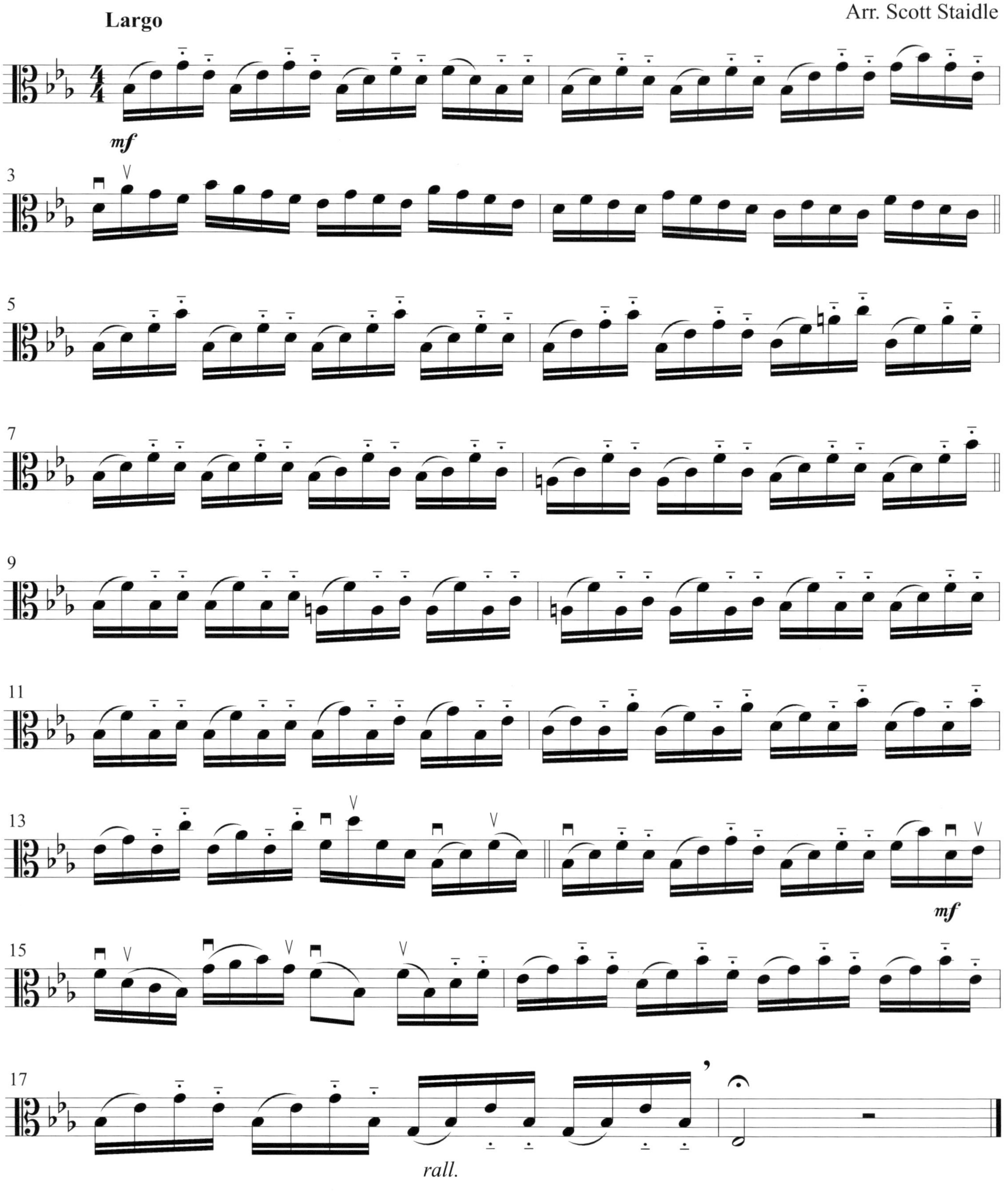

Largo

mf

3

5

7

9

11

13

mf

15

17

rall.

Other Mel Bay Viola Books

Concept and Study for the Viola: The Lobko Method
Modern Viola Method Grade 1 (Norgaard/Scott)
The American Fiddle Method for Viola Vol. 1 (Wicklund/Farr)
American Fiddle Tunes for Solo and Ensemble: Viola/Violin 3 (C. Duncan)
Celtic Fiddle Tunes for Solo and Ensemble: Viola/Violin 3 (C. Duncan)
Christmas Songs for Beginning Viola Level 1 (C. Duncan)
Christmas Strings: Viola/Violin 3 & Ensemble Score (Miller)
Classical Repertoire for Viola Vol. 1 (Puscoiu)
Easy Classics for Viola (Spitzer)
Easy Solos for Beginning Viola (C. Duncan)
Fiddling Classics for Solo & Ensemble: Viola/Violin 3 and Score (C. Duncan)
Fiddle Tunes for Two Violas (Phillips)
Fun with the Viola (W. Bay)
Hymns for Viola Made Easy (Clarke)
Jazz Viola Wizard Junior, Book 1 (Norgaard)
Jazz Viola Wizard Junior, Book 2 (Norgaard)
Music from Around the World for Solo & Ensemble: Viola/Violin 3 (Miller)
My Very Best Christmas: Viola (Khanagov)
Sacred Melodies for Solo Viola (C. Duncan)
Scottish Airs and Dances for Viola & Cello/or Solo Viola (Witt)
Scottish Fiddling for Viola (Witt)
Student's Book of Rounds: Viola (Worth)
The Student Violist: Bach (C. Duncan)
The Student Violist: Beethoven (C. Duncan)
The Student Violist: Handel (C. Duncan)
The Student Violist: Mozart (C. Duncan)
Wedding Music for Solo Viola (Curatolo)
Beginner Viola Theory for Children Book 1 (M. Smith)
Beginner Viola Theory for Children Book 2 (M. Smith)
Beginner Viola Theory for Children Book 3 (M. Smith)
Speed Reading for Viola (Bauer)
Viola Wall Chart (Norgaard)

WWW.MELBAY.COM

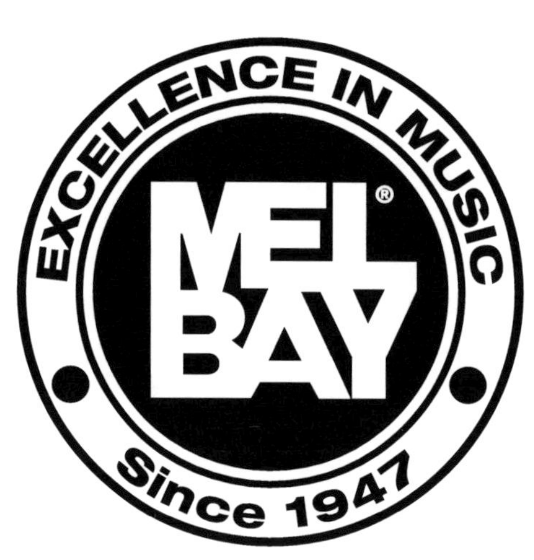
EXCELLENCE IN MUSIC
MEL BAY
Since 1947

WEDDING MUSIC FOR VIOLIN AND VIOLA

by Scott Staidle

VIOLIN

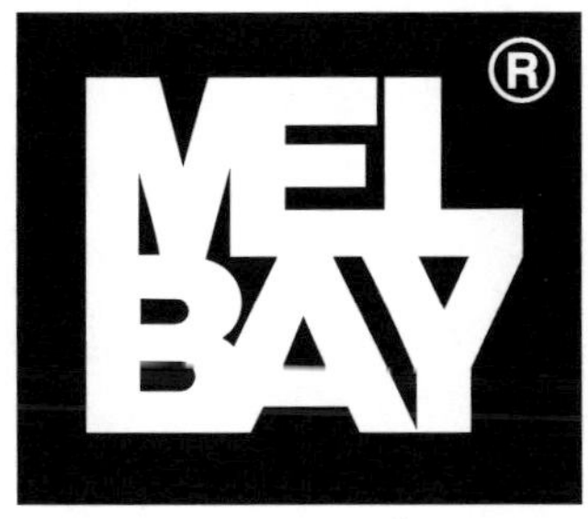

WWW.MELBAY.COM

Contents

Title	Page

Air in "D"
for Violin and Viola

Violin

J. S. Bach
Arr. Scott Staidle

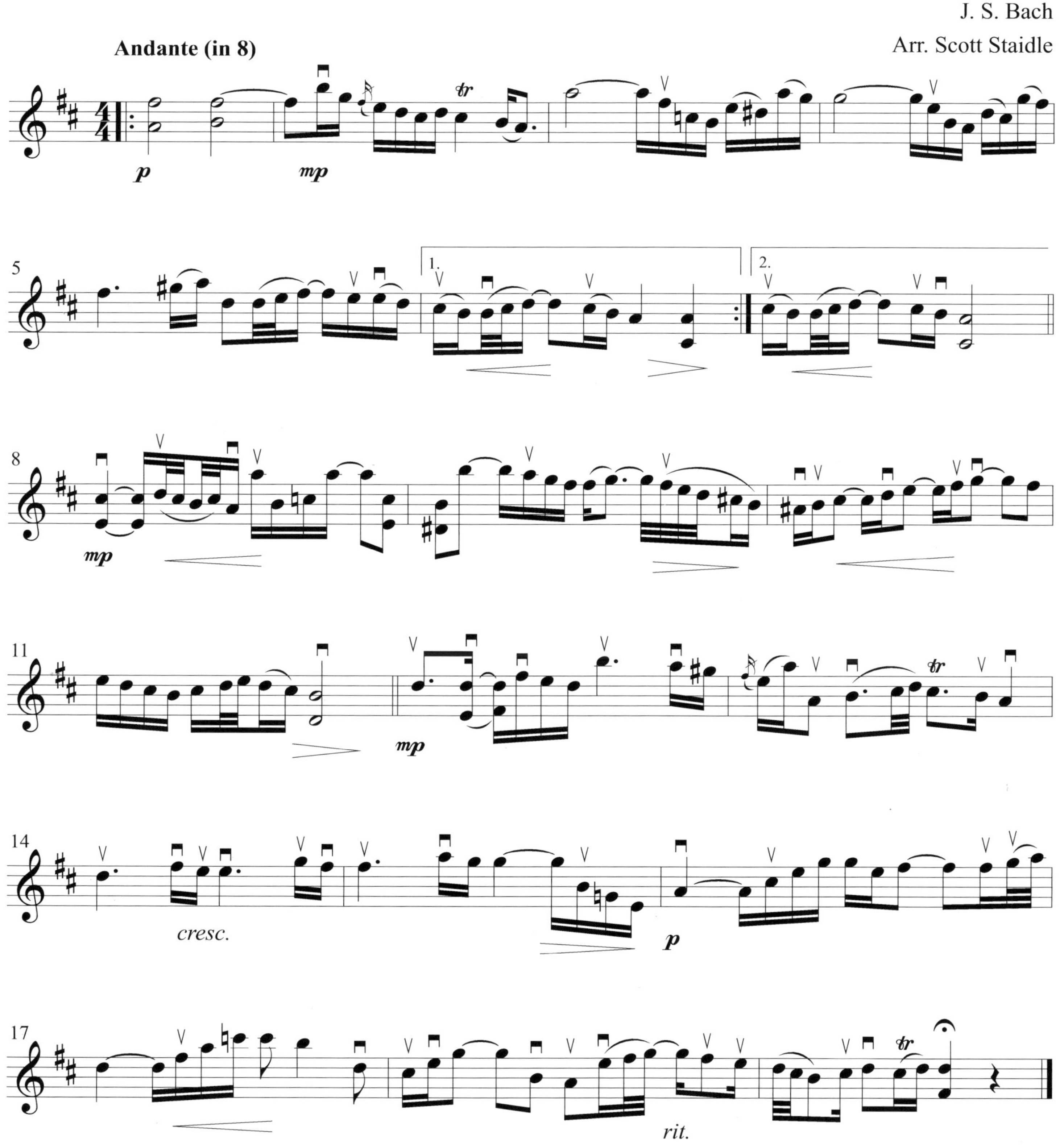

Allegro
for Violin and Viola

Violin

J. H. Fiocco
Arr. Scott Staidle

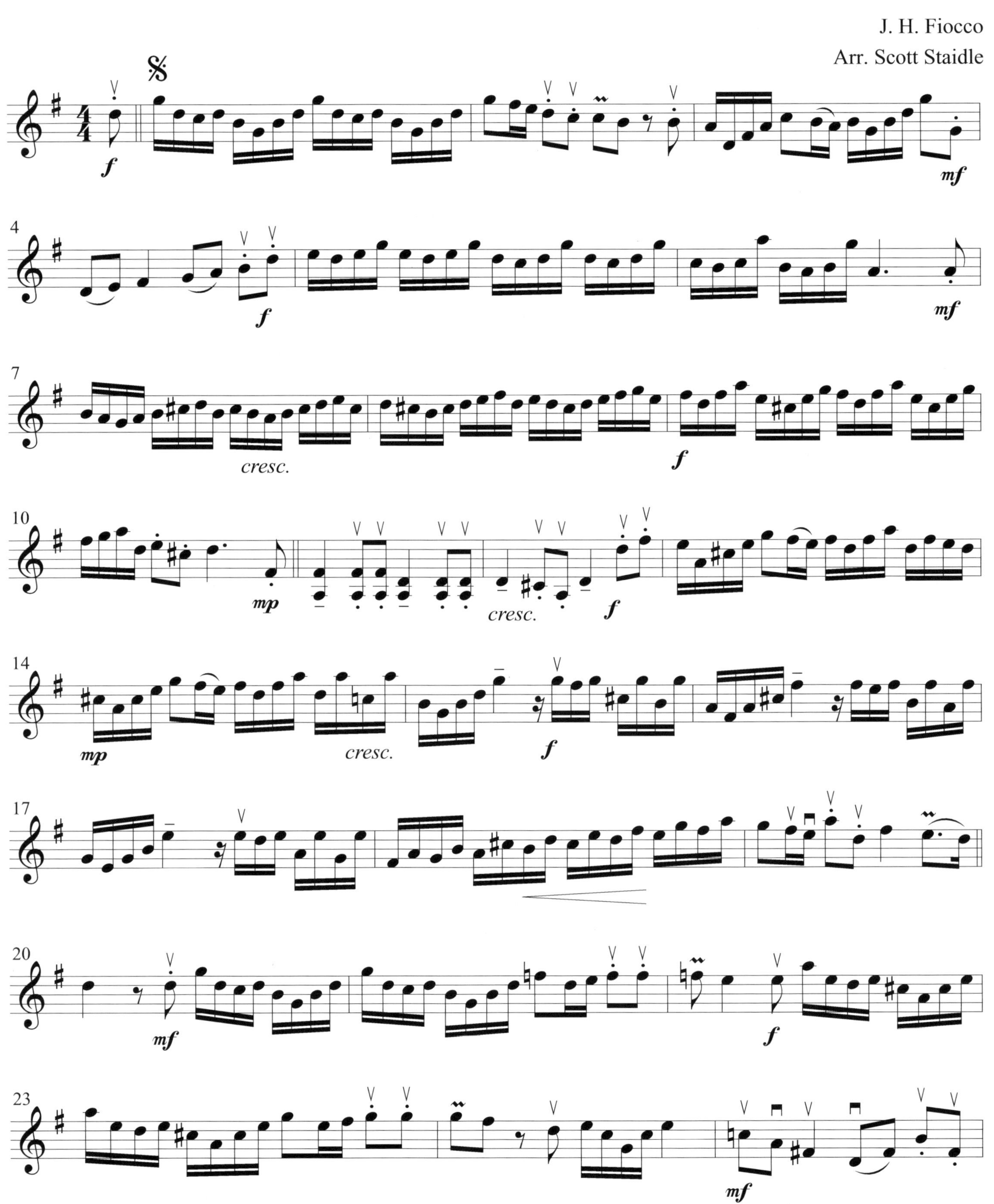

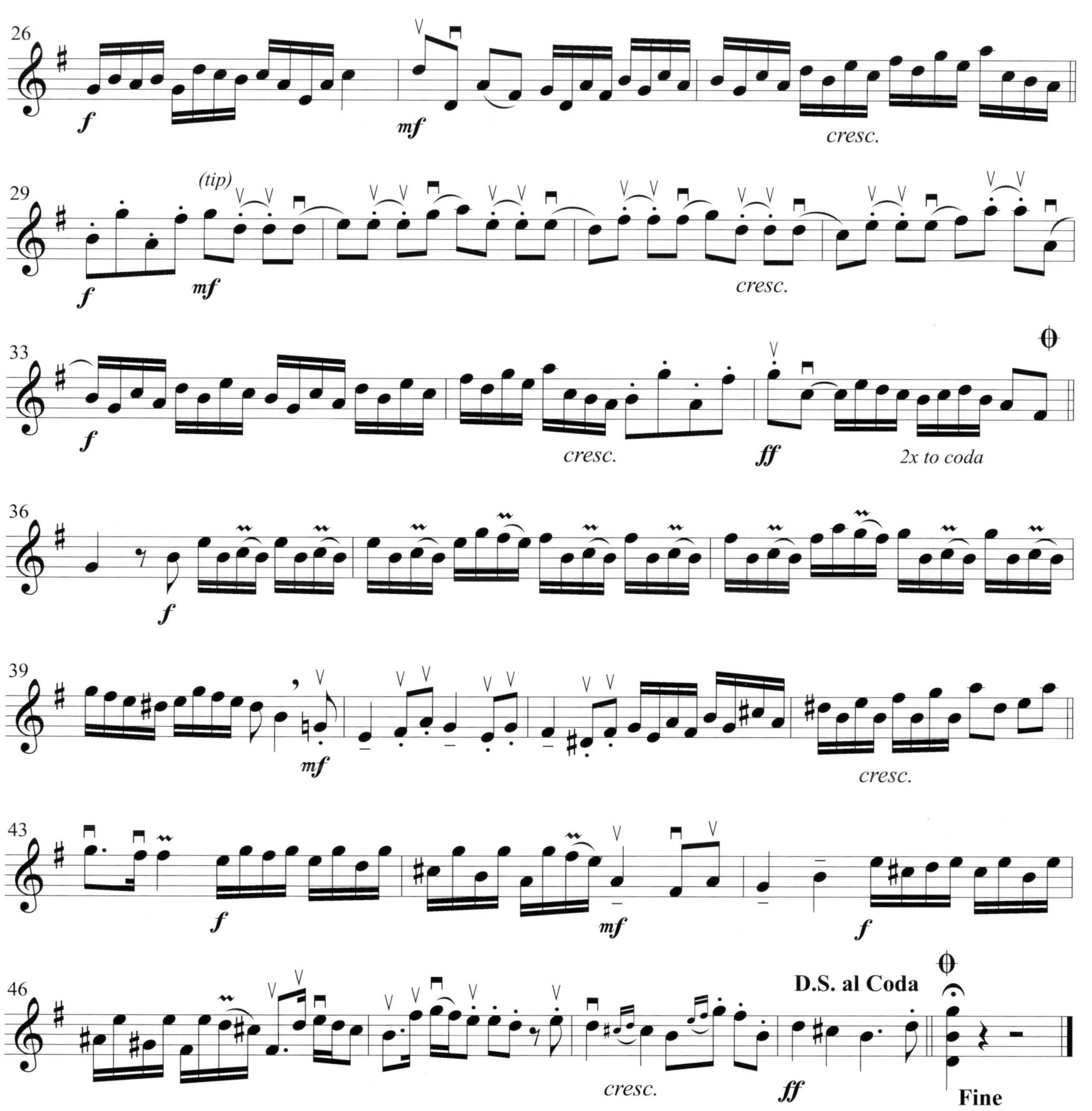
26
f
mf
cresc.
29
(tip)
f
mf
cresc.
33
f
cresc.
ff
2x to coda
36
f
39
mf
cresc.
43
f
mf
f
46
D.S. al Coda
cresc.
ff
Fine

Amazing Grace
for Violin and Viola

Violin

Traditional
Arr. Scott Staidle

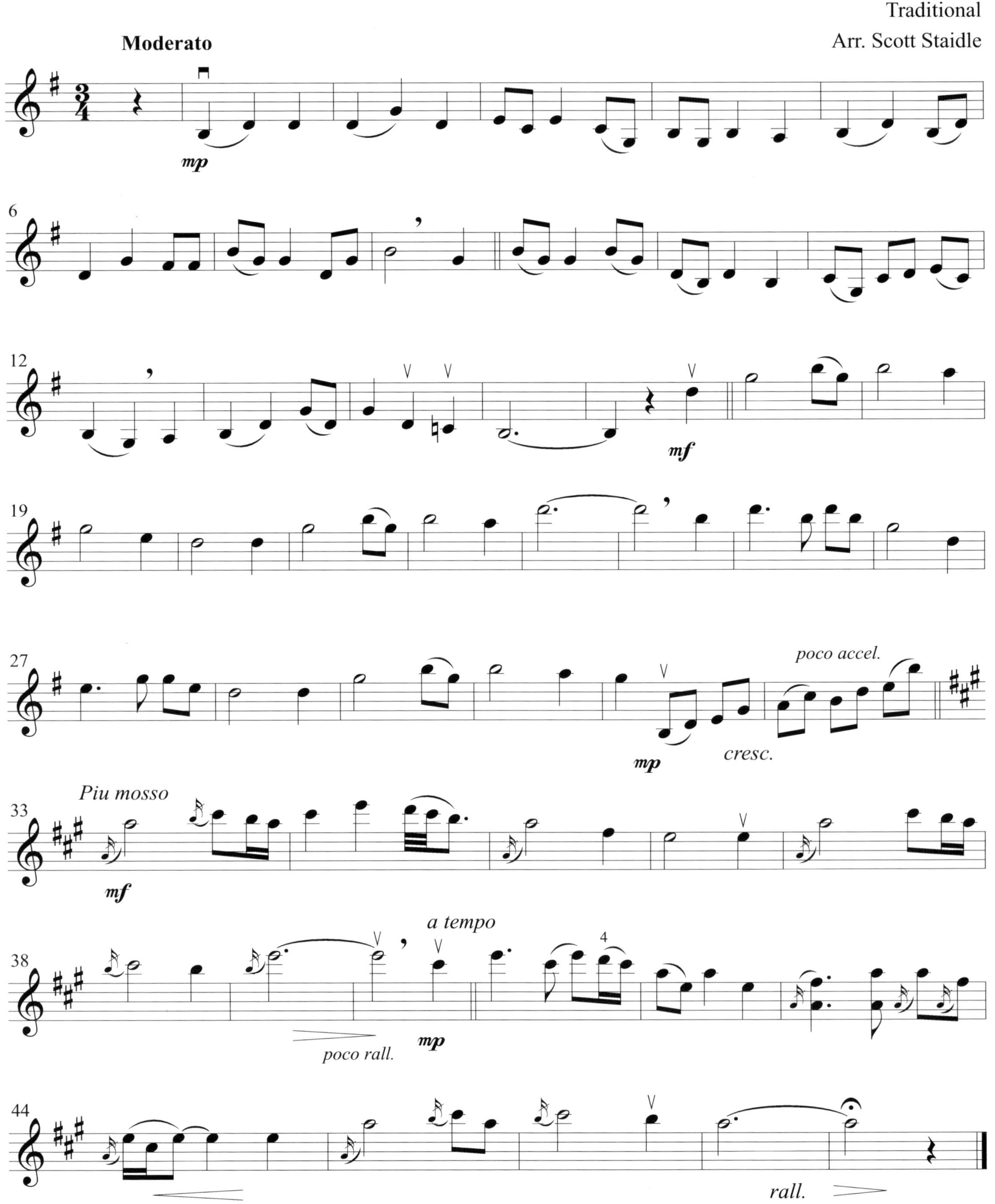

Jesu, Joy of Man's Desiring
for Violin and Viola

Violin

J. S. Bach
Arr. Scott Staidle

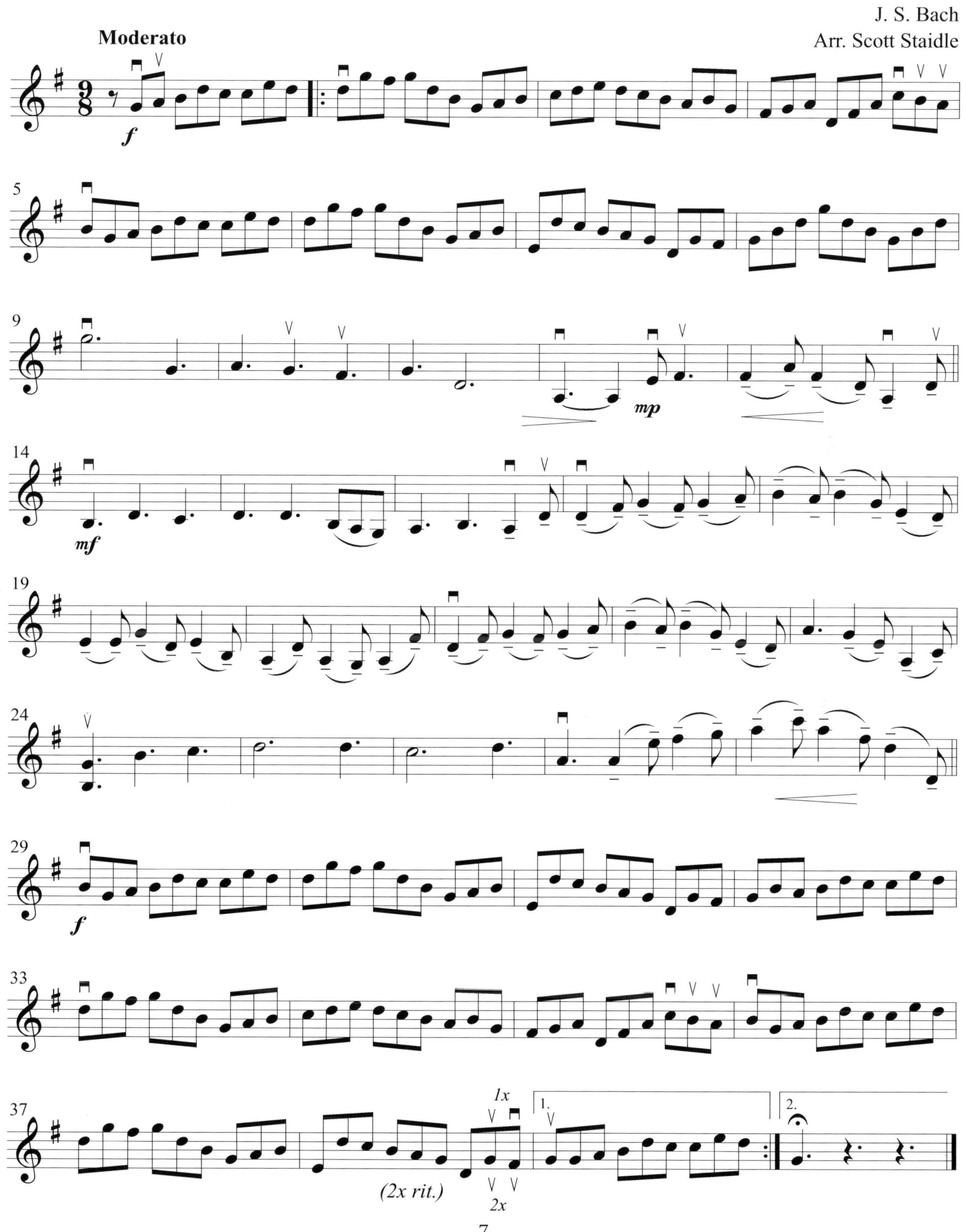

Kanon
for Violin and Viola

Violin

J. Pachelbel
Arr. Scott Staidle

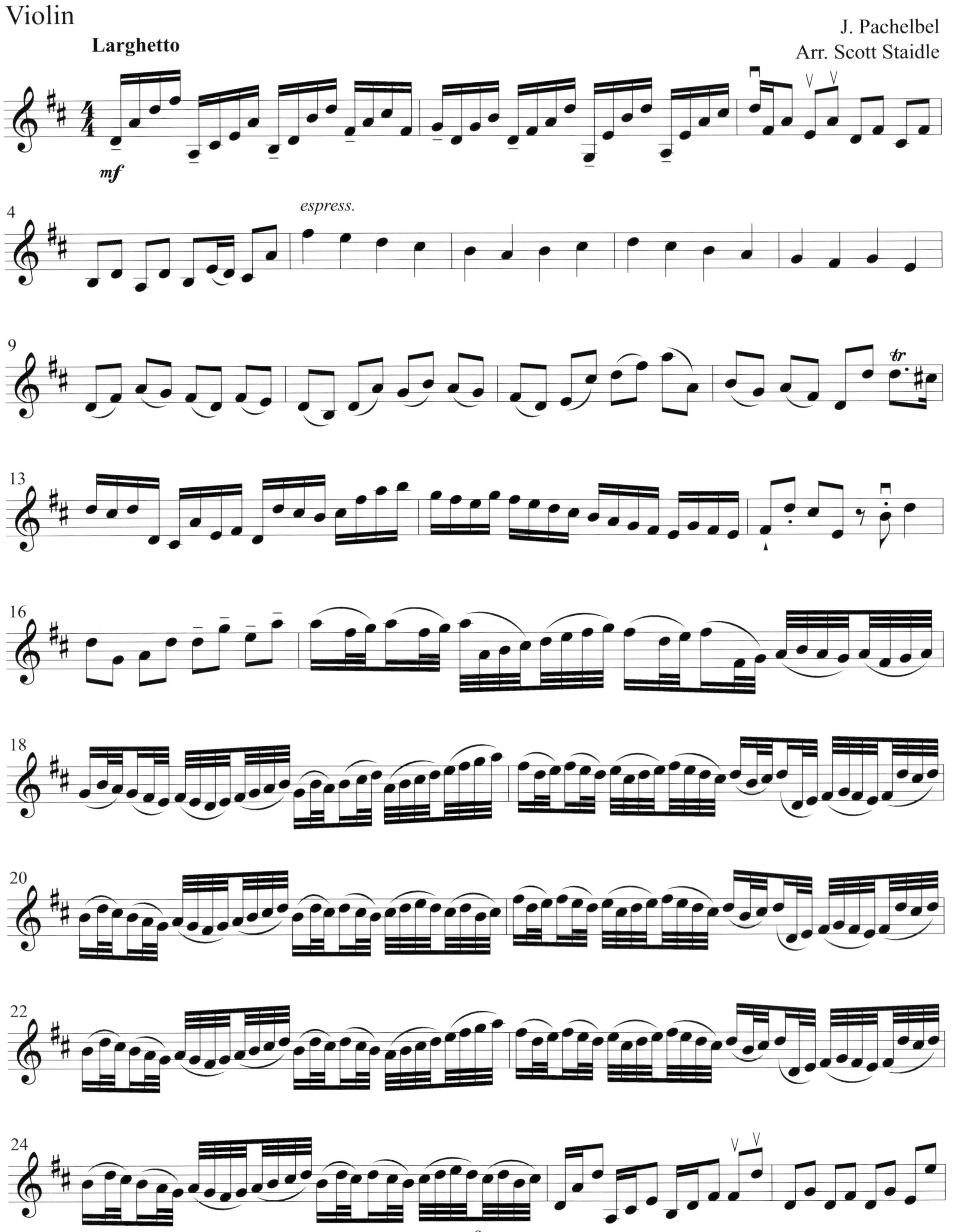

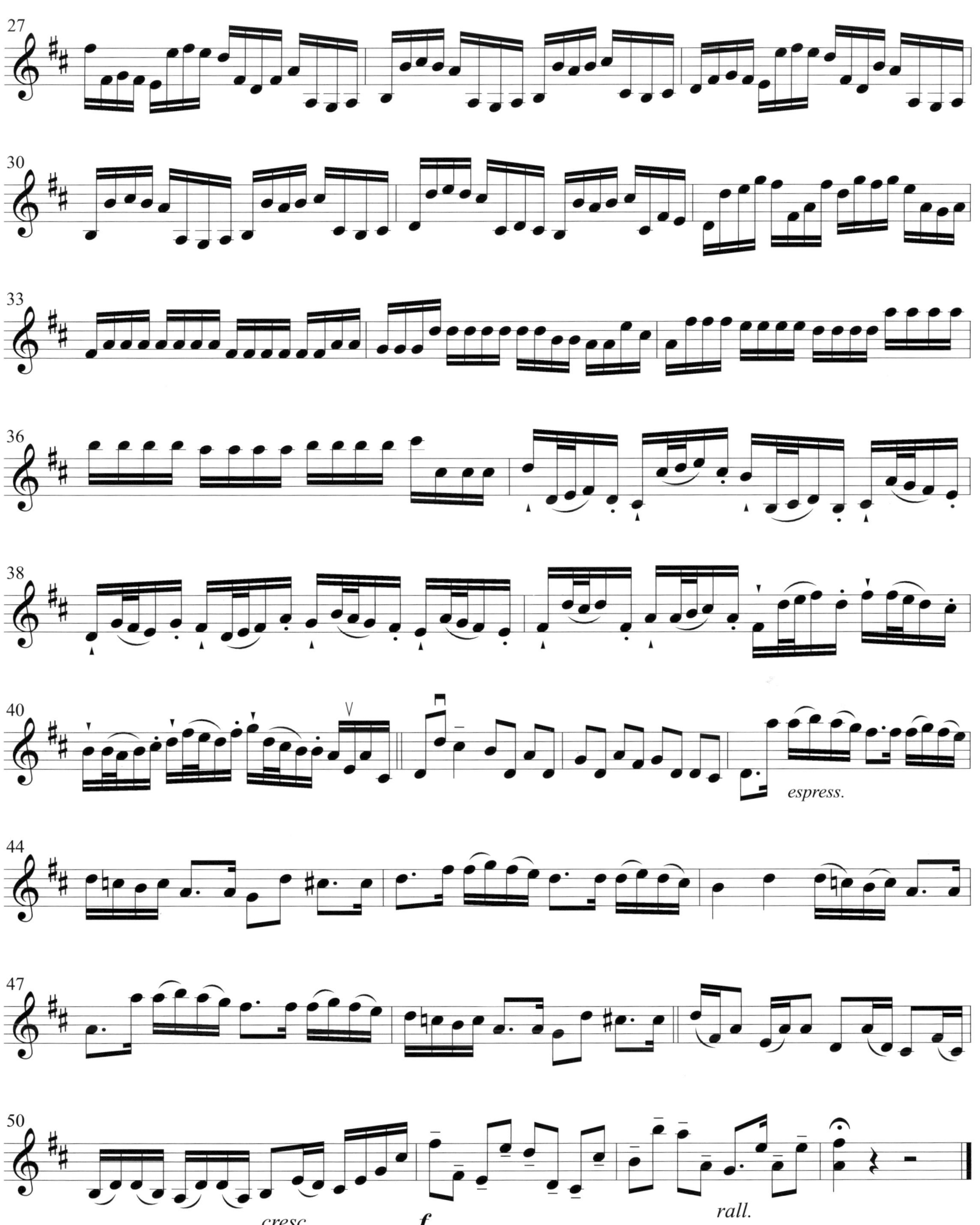
27
30
33
36
38
40
espress.
44
47
50
cresc.
f
rall.

Bridal Chorus
for Violin and Viola

Violin

R. Wagner
Arr. Scott Staidle

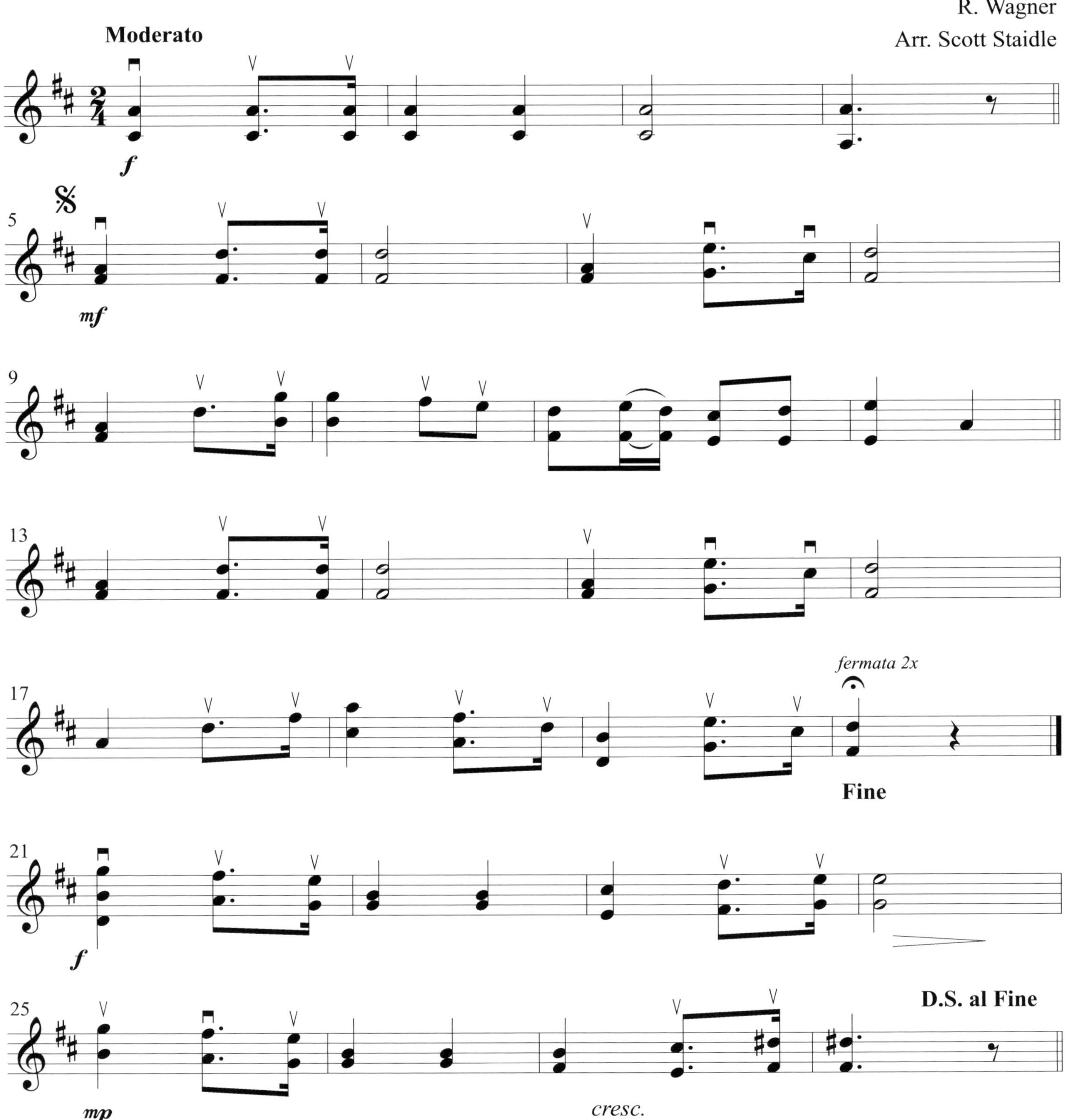

This page is left blank to avoid an awkward page turn.

Menuetto
for Violin and Viola

Violin

L. Boccherini
Arr. Scott Staidle

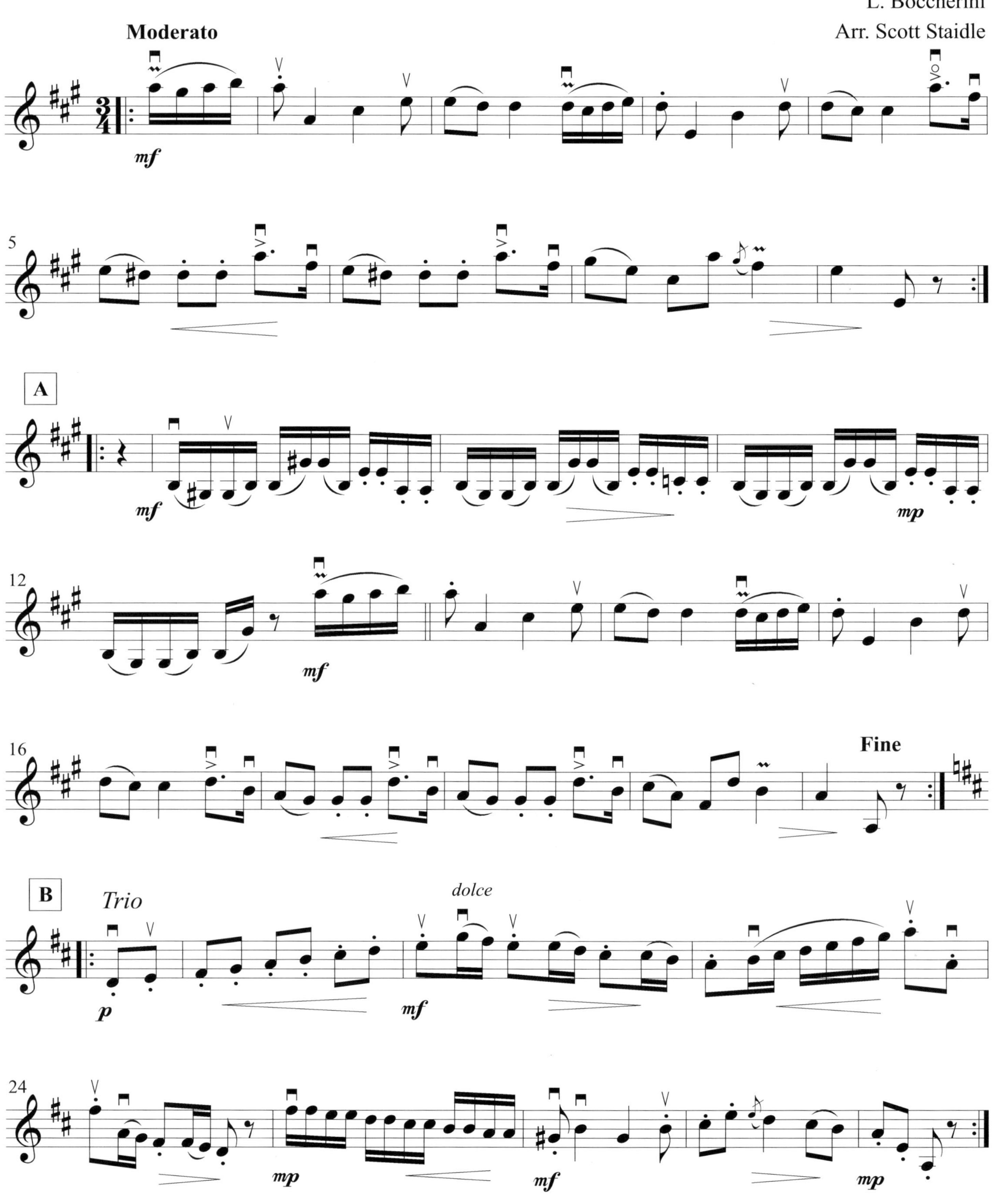

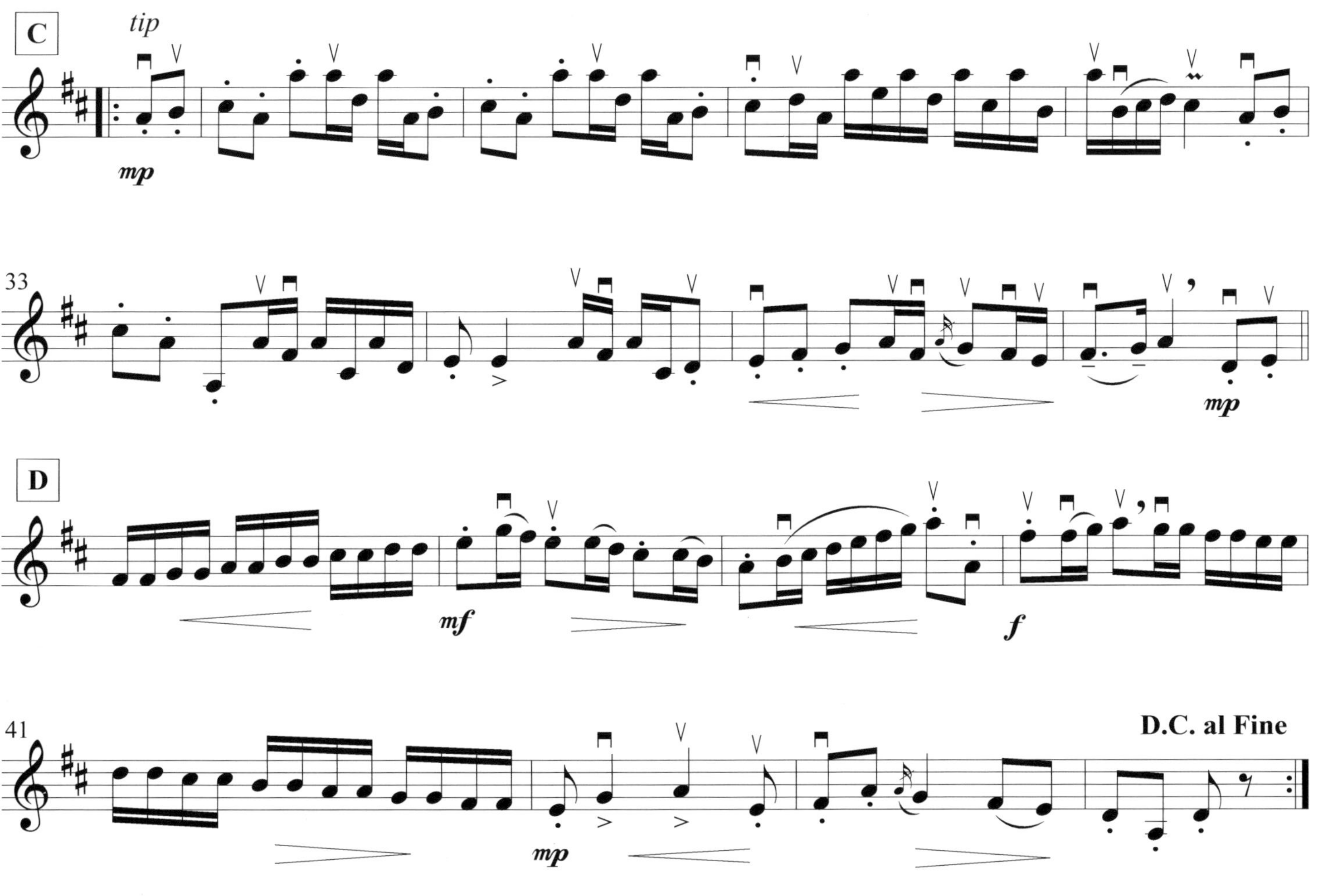
C
tip
mp
33
mp
D
mf
f
41
D.C. al Fine
mp

Ode to Joy

for Violin and Viola

Violin

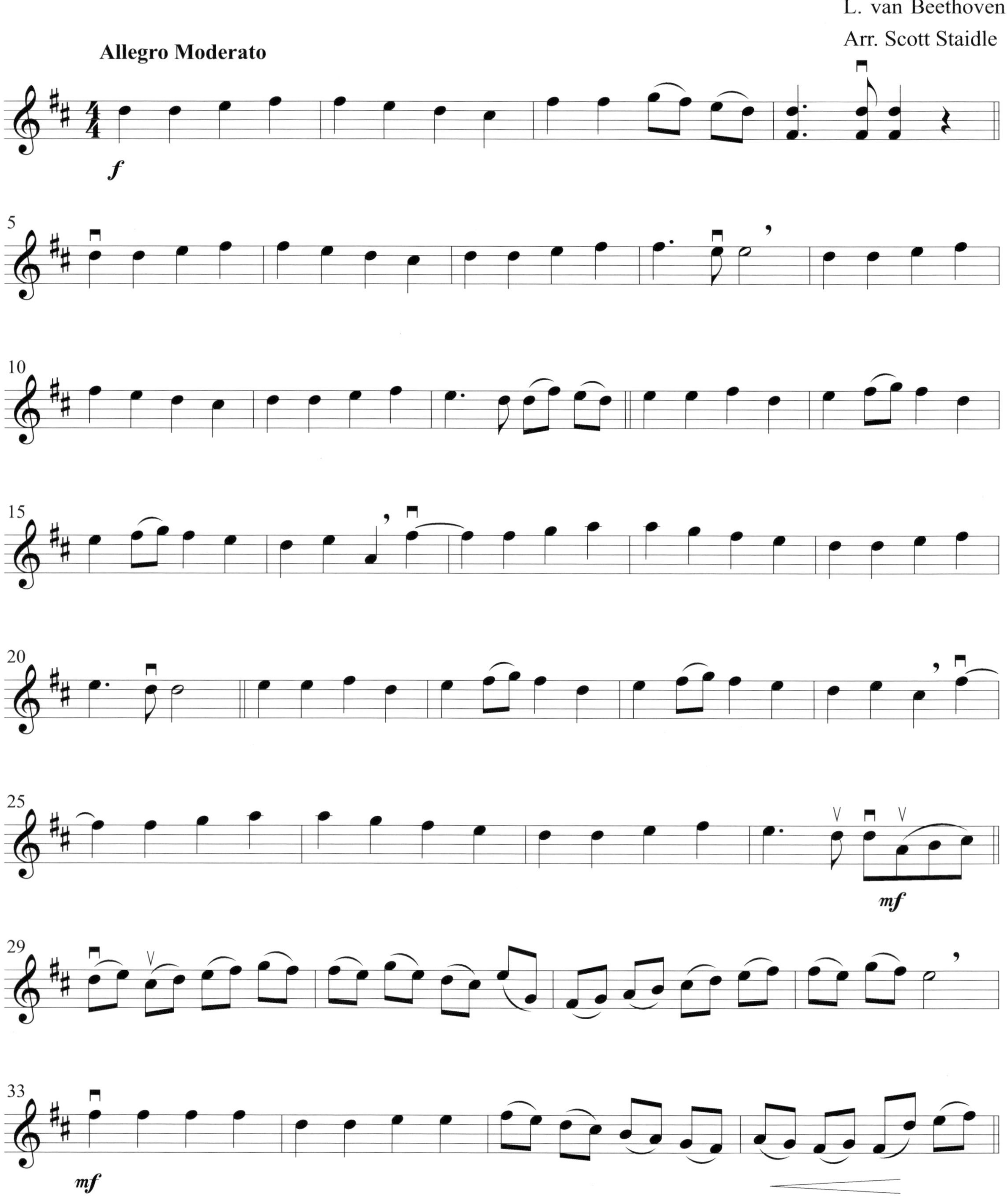

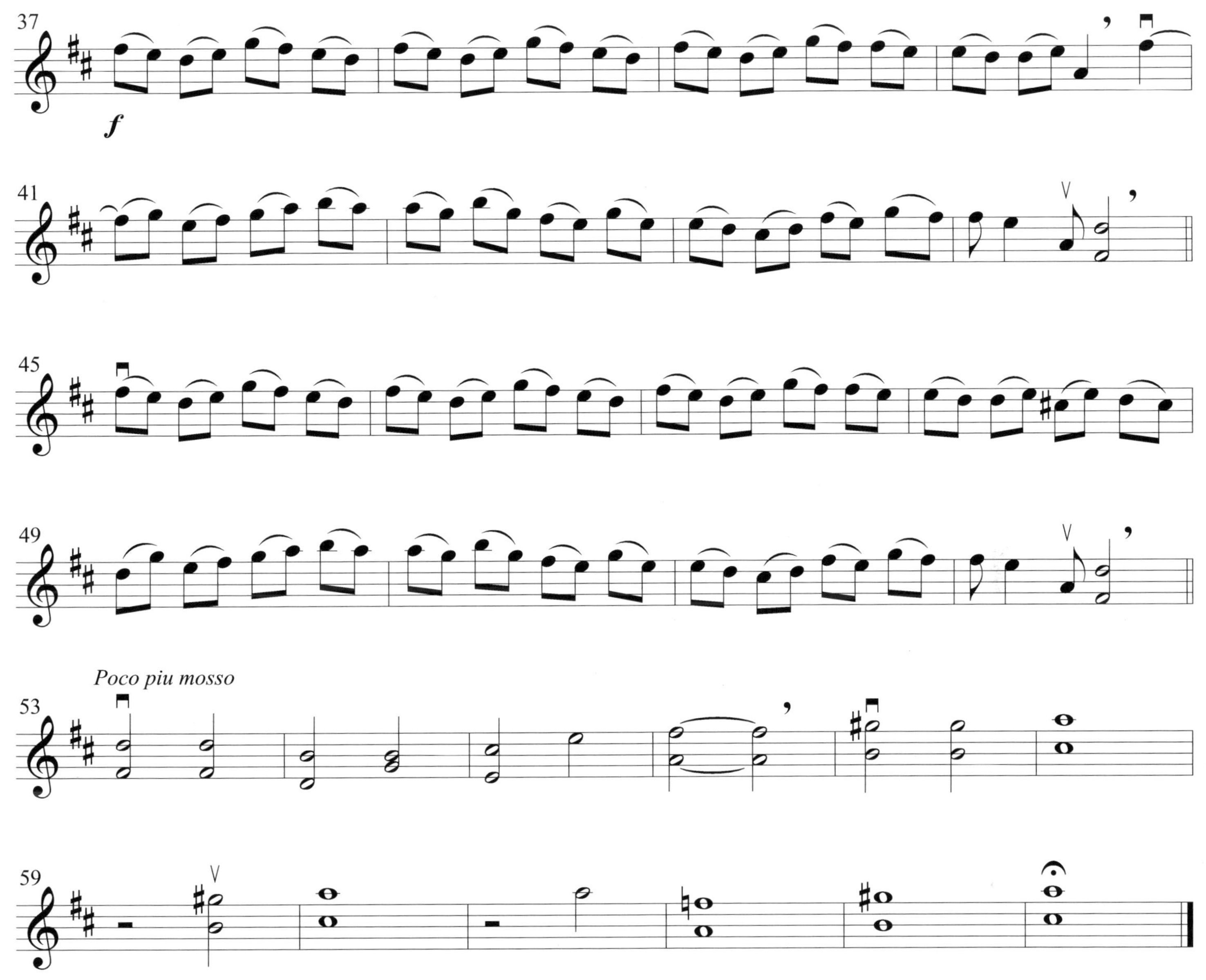

Poco piu mosso

Trumpet Voluntary in "D"
for Violin and Viola

Violin

H. Purcell
Arr. Scott Staidle

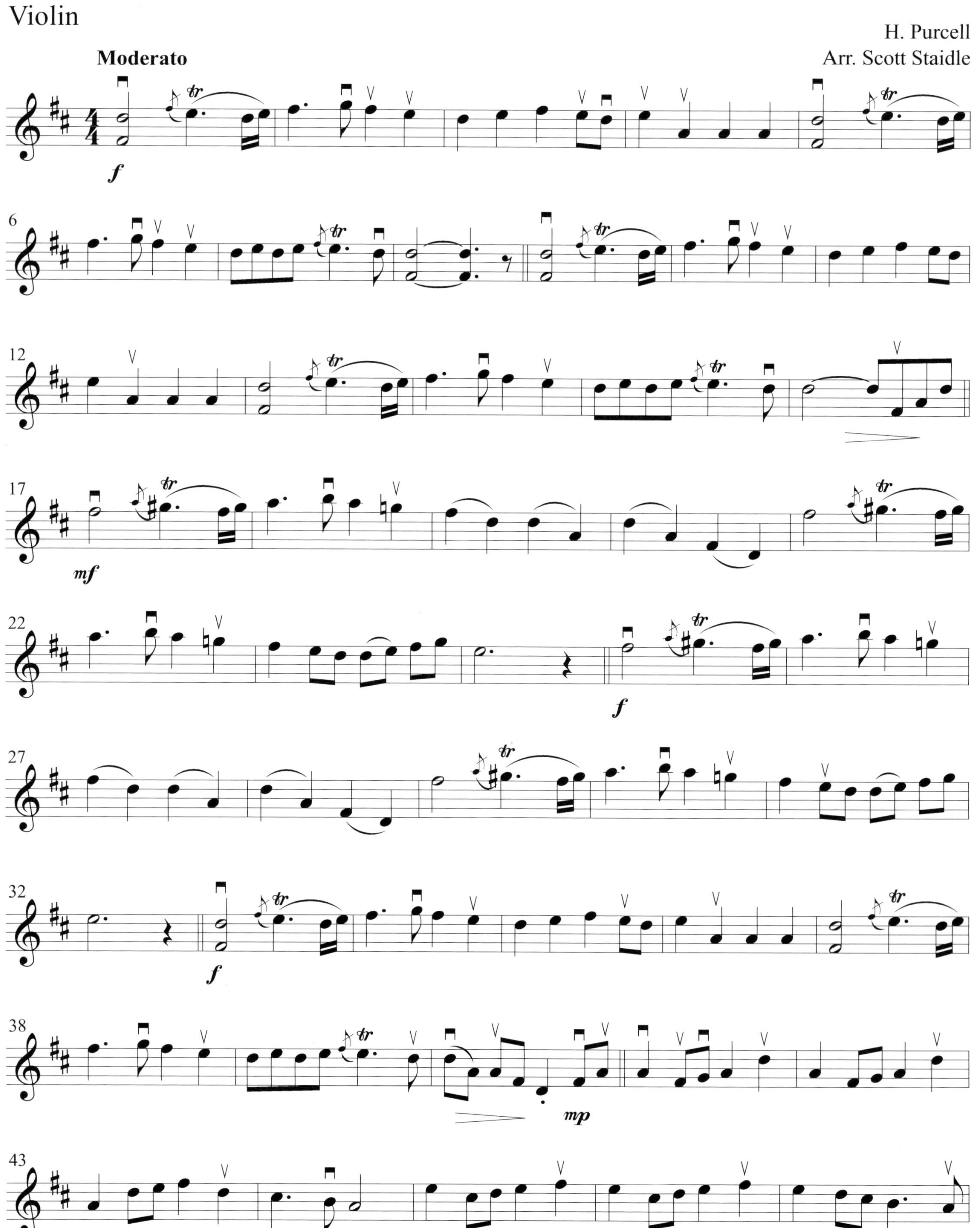

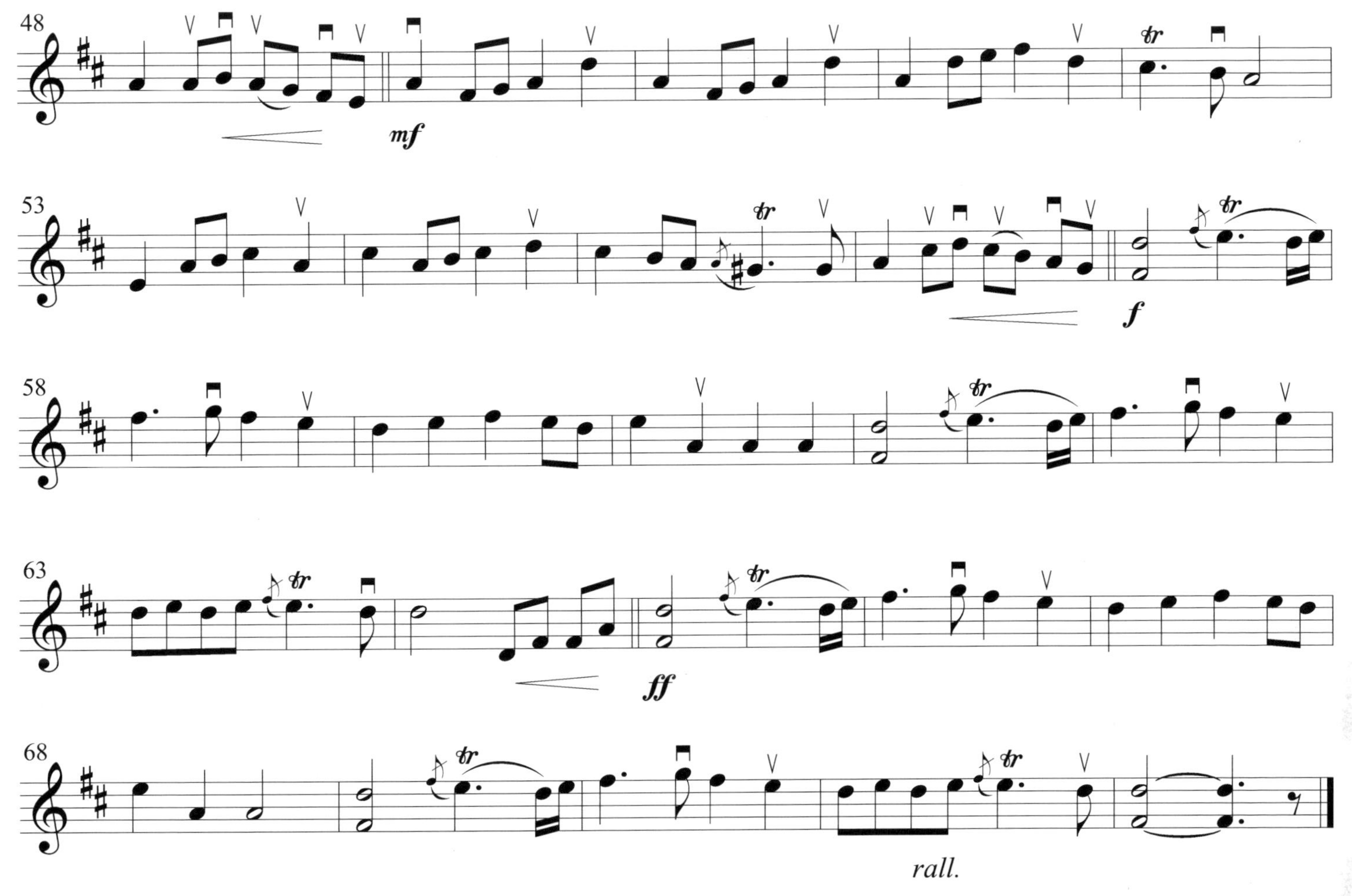
48
mf
53
f
58
63
ff
68
rall.

Wedding March
for Violin and Viola

Violin

F. Mendelssohn
Arr. Scott Staidle

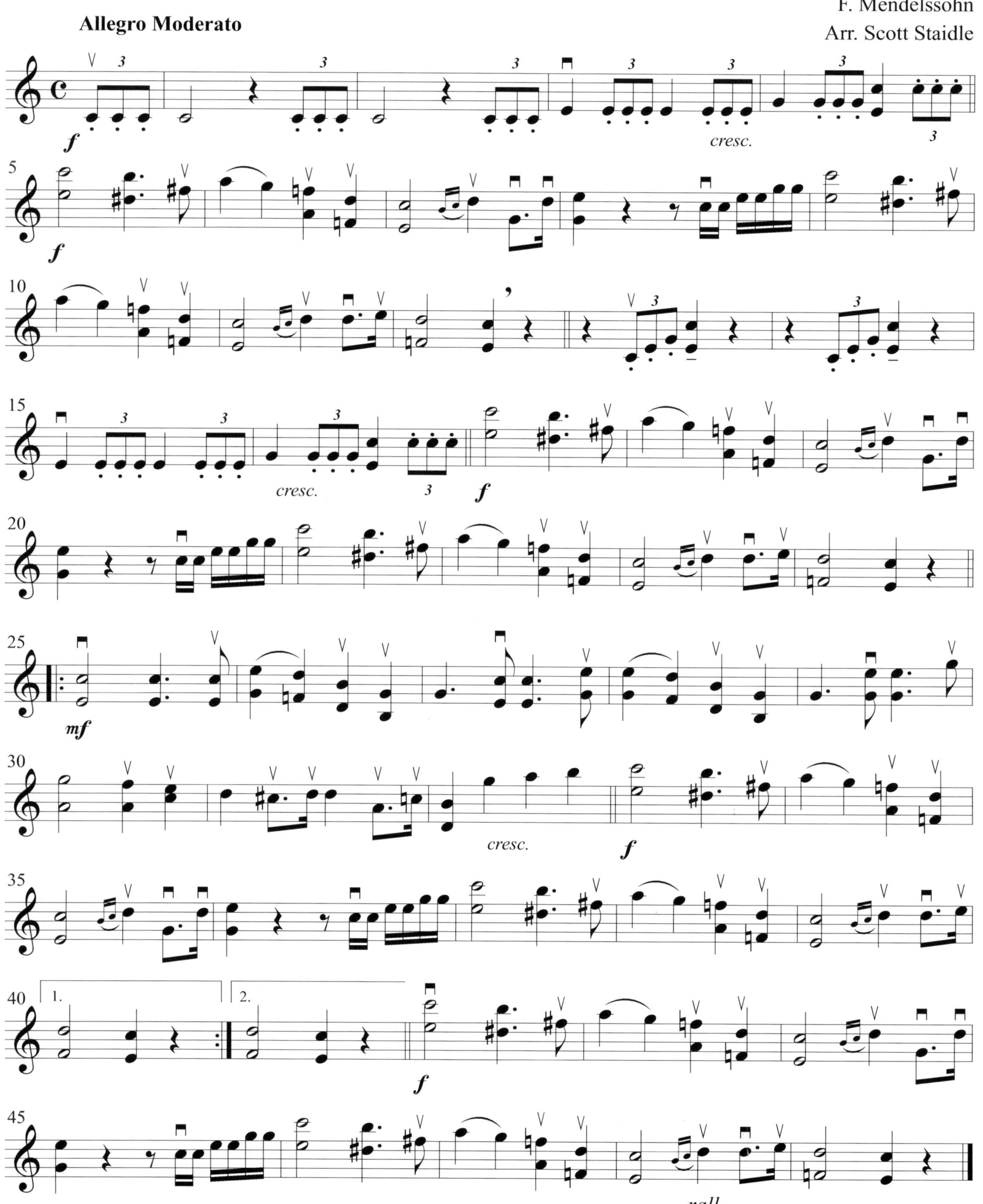

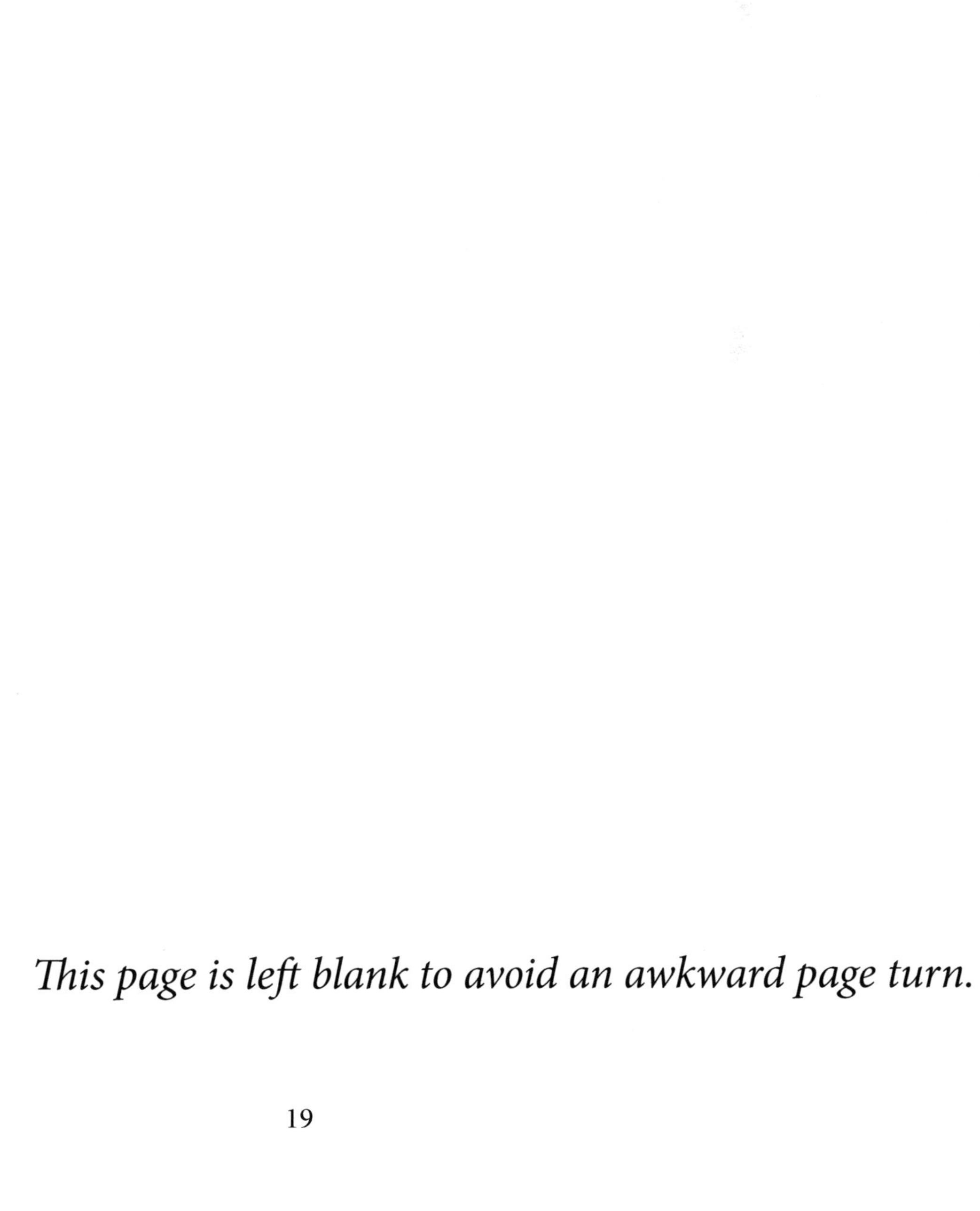

This page is left blank to avoid an awkward page turn.

Violin

Rondeau

for Violin and Viola

J. Mouret
Arr. Scott Staidle

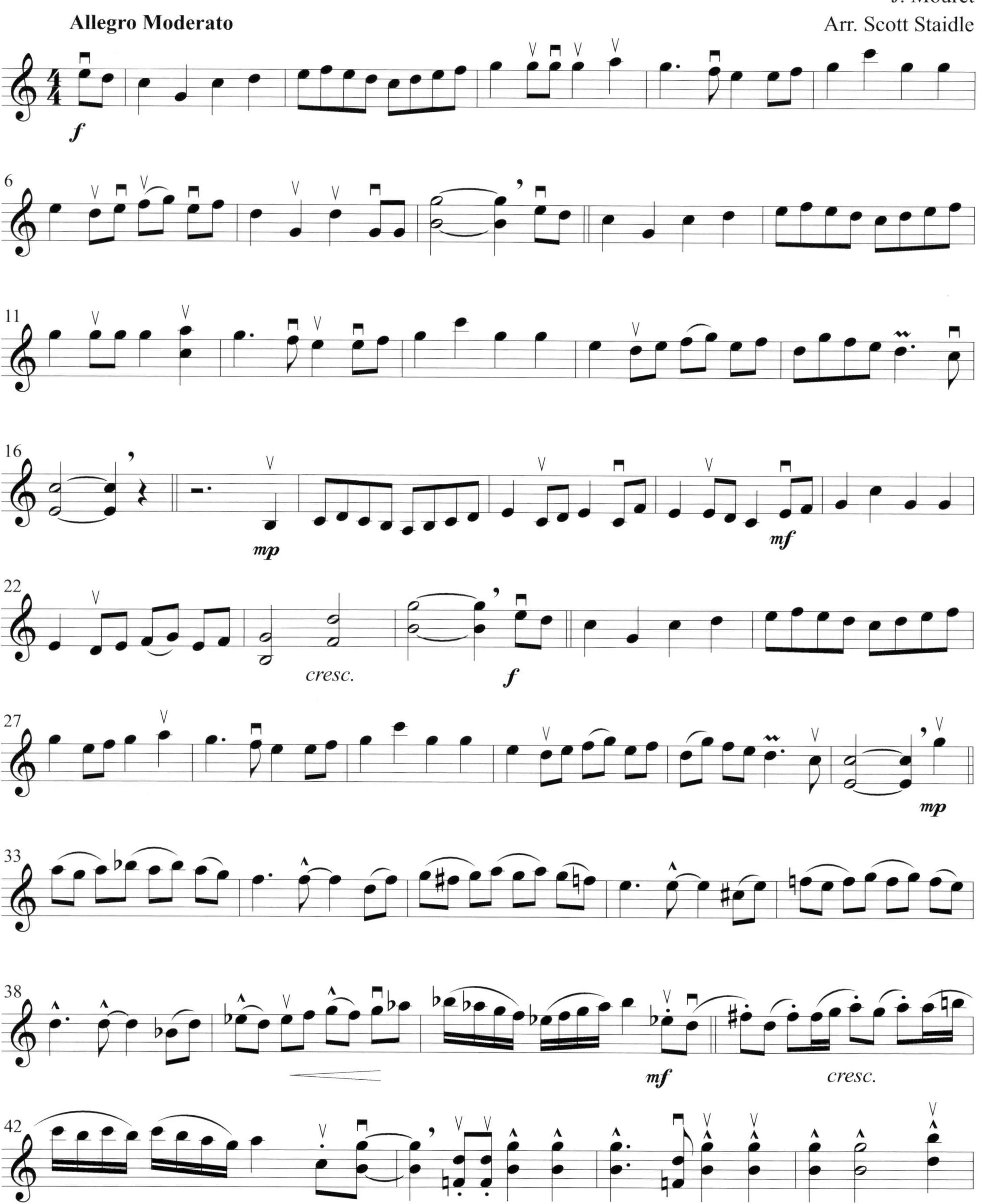

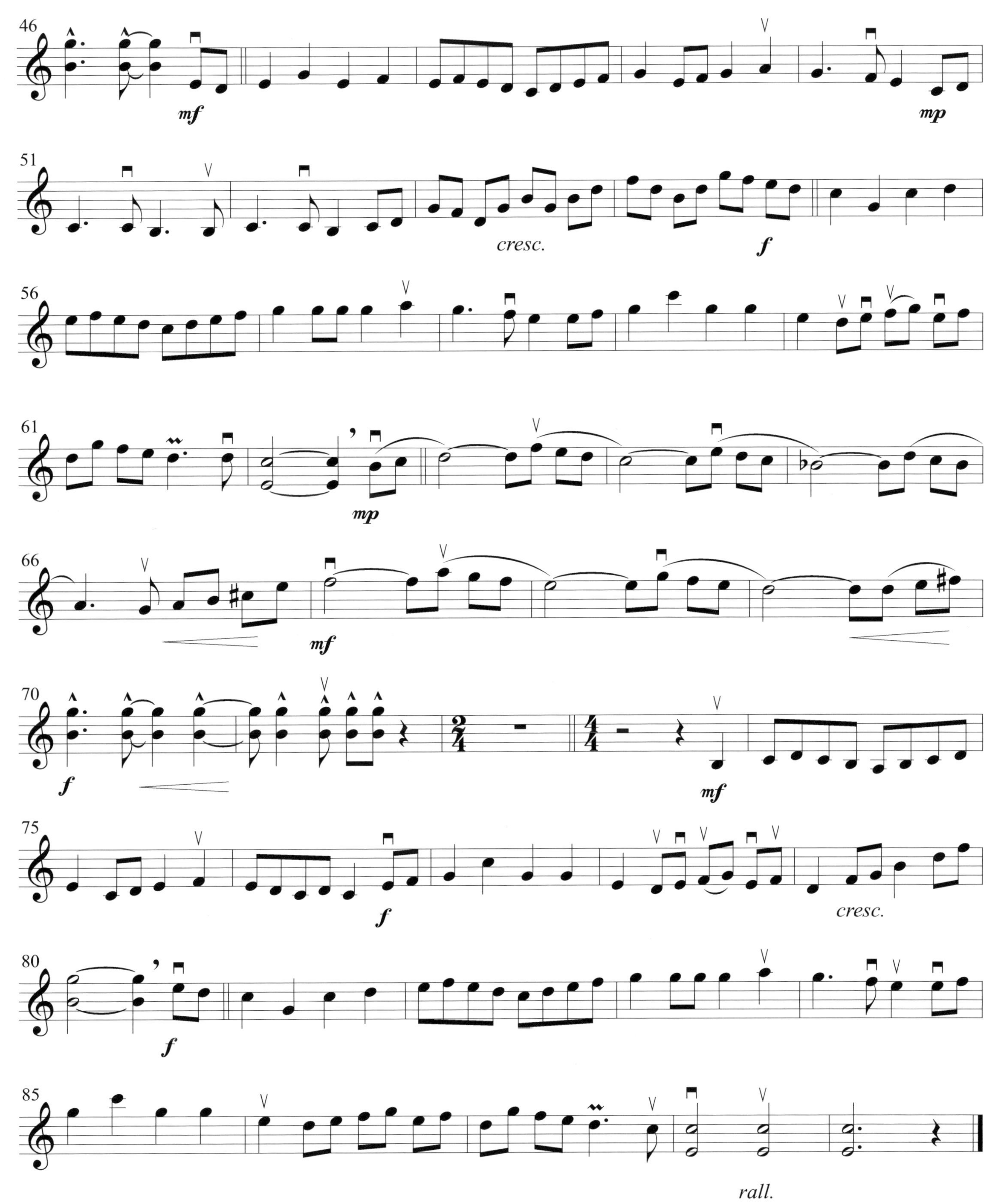
46
mf
mp
51
cresc.
f
56
61
mp
66
mf
70
f
mf
75
f
cresc.
80
f
85
rall.

Serenade
for Violin and Viola

Violin

J. Haydn
Arr. Scott Staidle

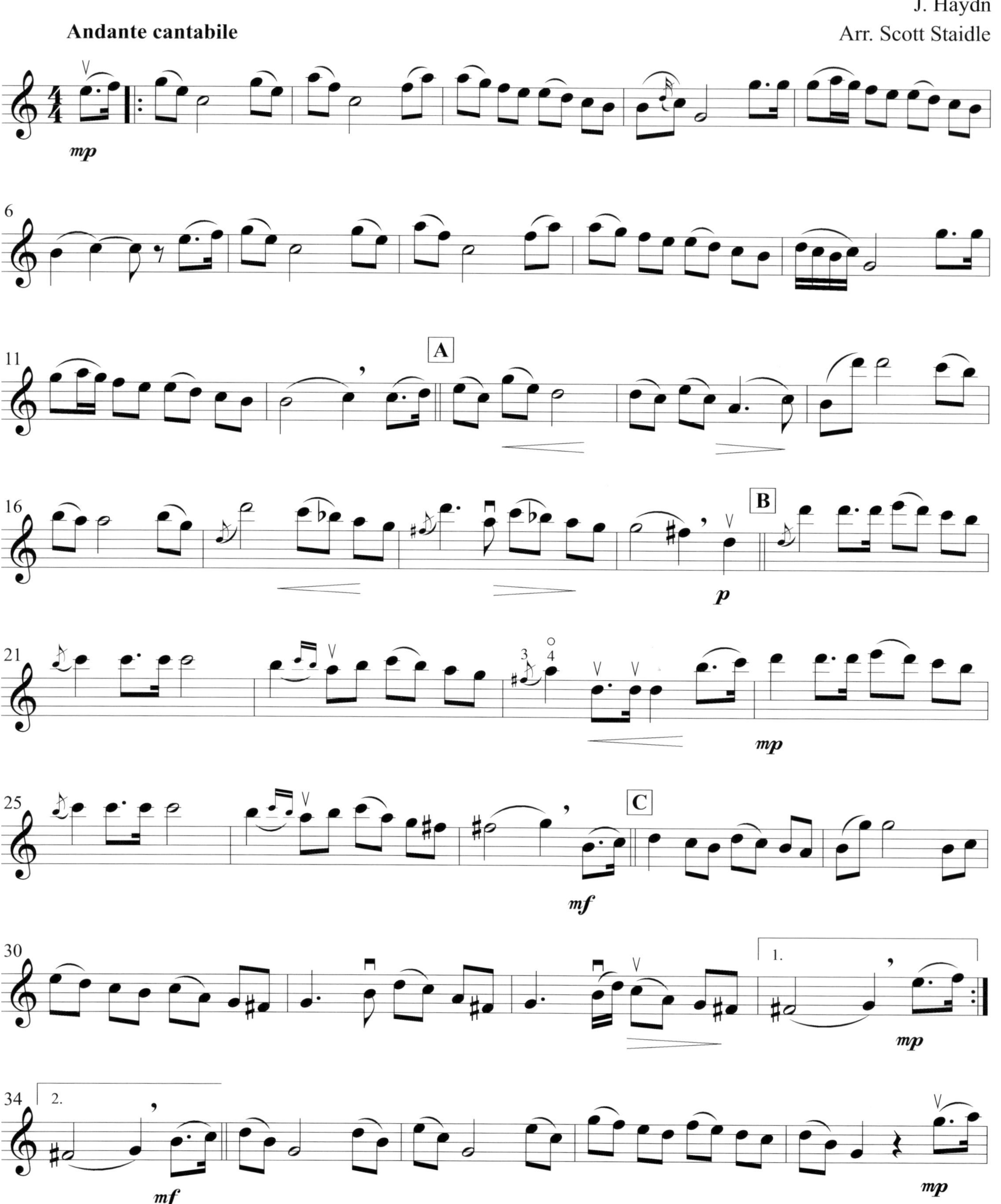

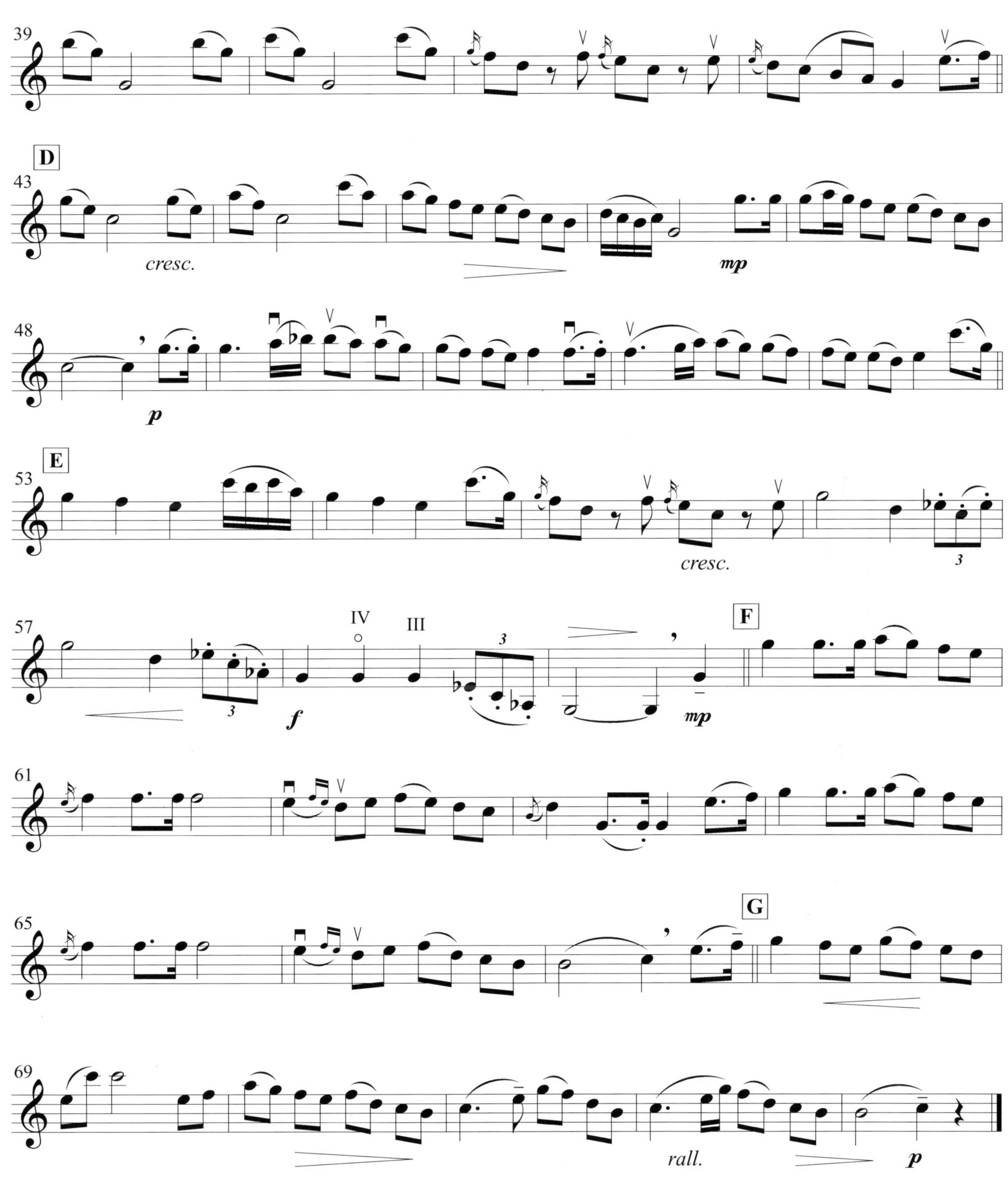

39
D
43
cresc.
mp
48
p
E
53
cresc.
3
57
3
f
IV
III
3
mp
F
61
65
G
69
rall.
p

Water Music - Hornpipe
for Violin and Viola

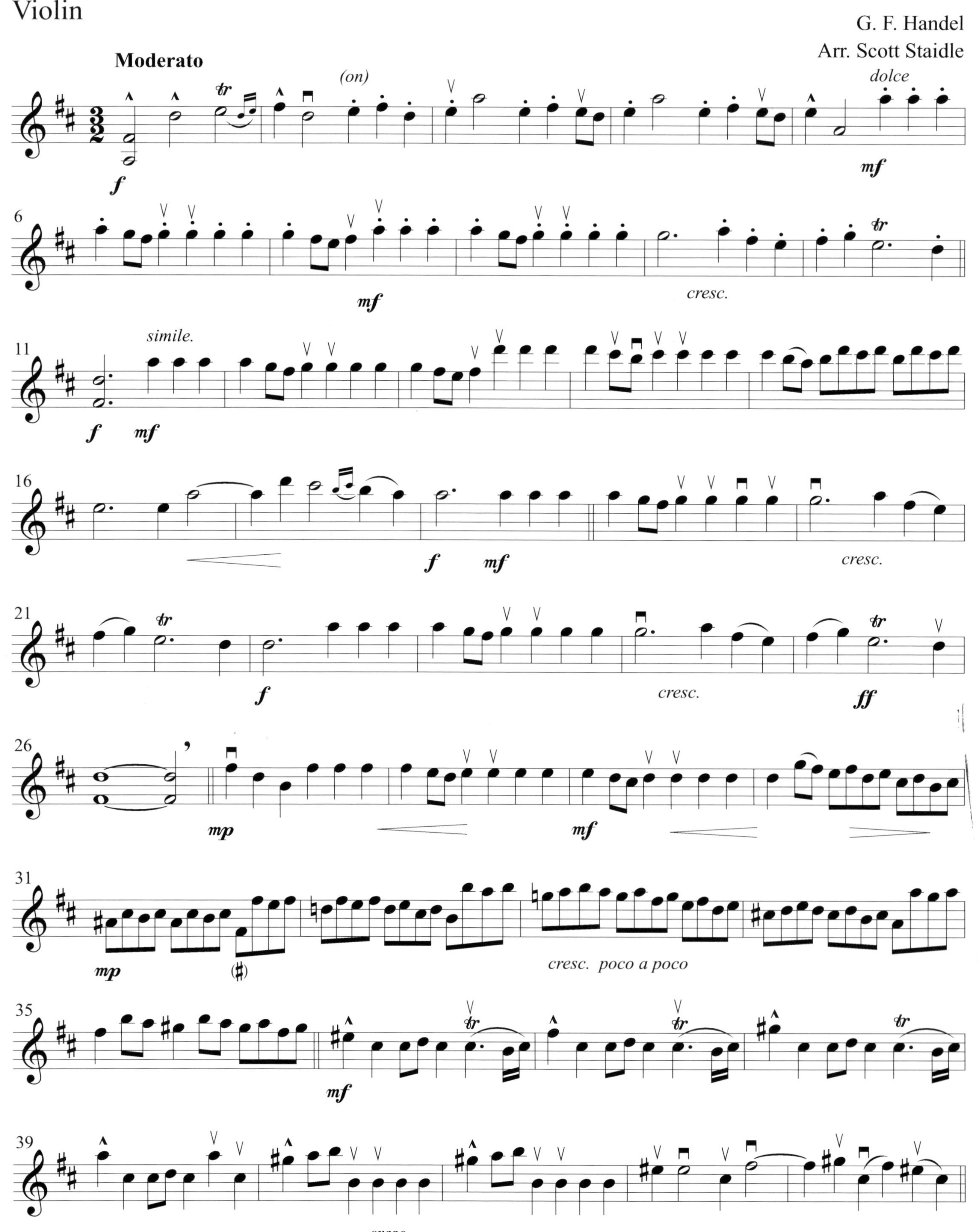

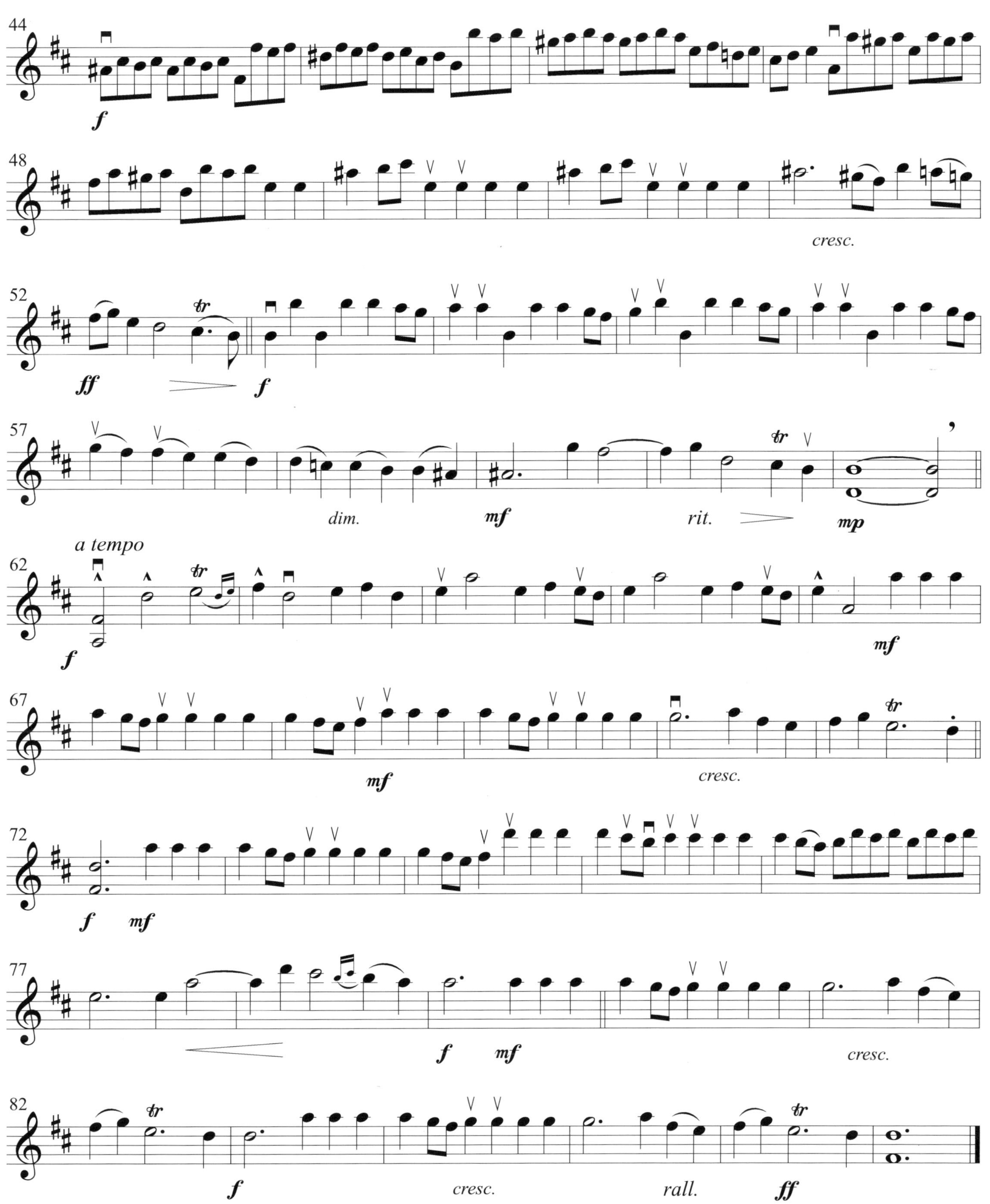
44
f
48
cresc.
52
ff
f
57
dim.
mf
rit.
mp
a tempo
62
f
mf
67
mf
cresc.
72
f
mf
77
f
mf
cresc.
82
f
cresc.
rall.
ff

Winter - 2nd Movement from "The Four Seasons"

for Violin and Viola

Violin

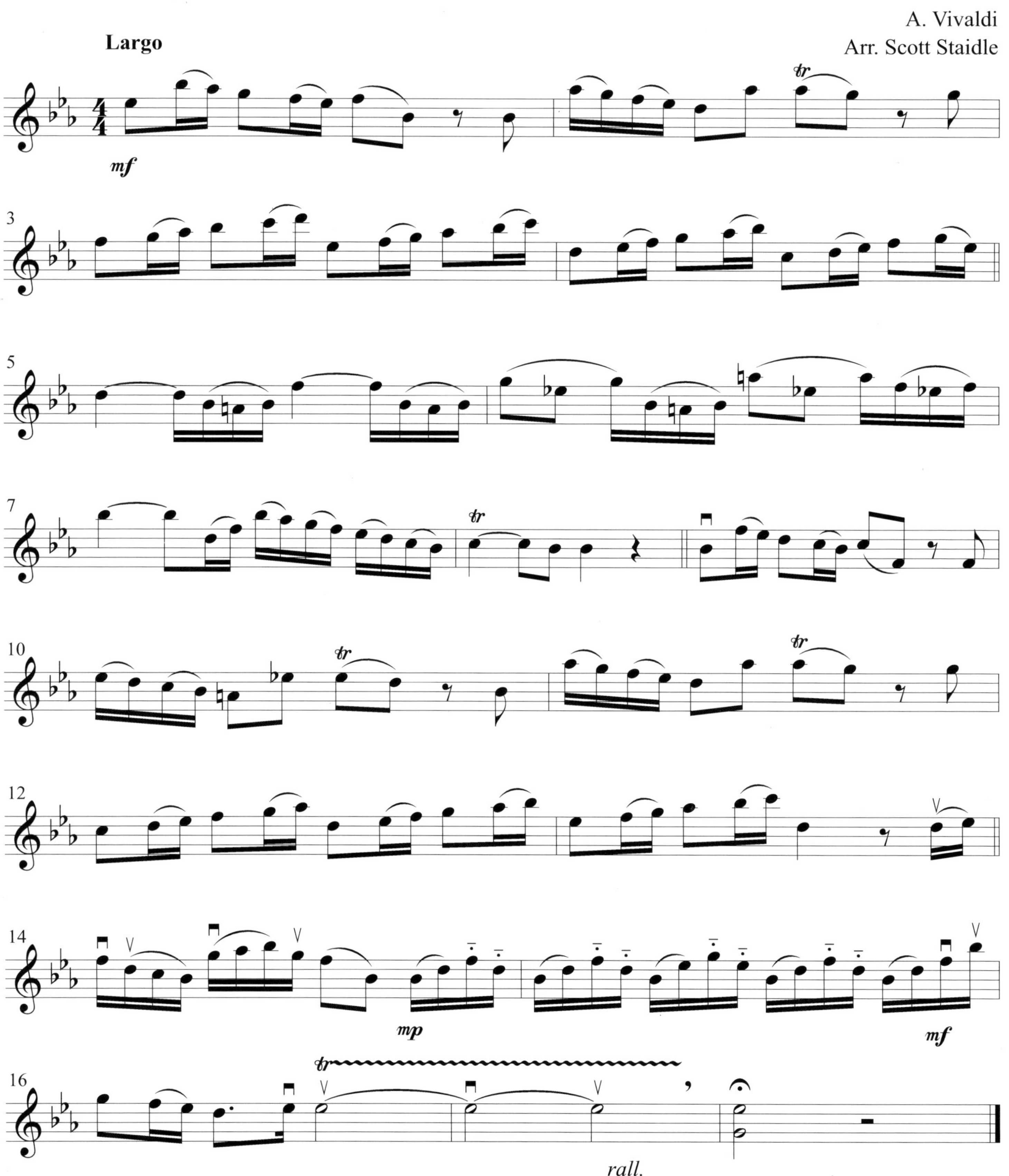

Other Mel Bay Violin Books

Violin Duets and String Ensembles

American Fiddle Tunes for Solo & Ensemble: Violins 1 & 2 (C. Duncan)
Celtic Fiddle Tunes for Solo & Ensemble: Violins 1 & 2 (C. Duncan)
Christmas Music Arranged for Violin Duet (Staidle)
Christmas Strings: Violin 1 & 2 with Piano Accompaniment (Miller)
Come Fiddle with Me Volume 1 (Hay)
Come Fiddle with Me Volume 2 (Hay)
Eastern European Music for Violin Duet (Harbar)
Easy Duets for Violin (Puscoiu)
Easy Violin Duets in First Position (Isaac)
Fiddling Classics for Solo & Ensemble: Violins 1 & 2 (C. Duncan)
J. S. Bach: Duets for Two Violins (Spencer/Engle)
Jazz Duets: Violin Edition (Biondi)
Music from Around the World for Solo & Ensemble: Violins 1 & 2 (Miller)
Ragtimes for Two Violins (Brydern)
Scottish Airs and Dances for Two Violins (Witt)
Scottish Melodies for Two Violins (Witt)
Twin Fiddling (Phillips)
Violin Duet Classics Made Playable (Harbar)
Wedding Music for Two Violins (Staidle)

Violin Scales, Study and Technique

Complete Violin Scale Dictionary (Isaac)
Concept and Study for the Violinist (Lobko)
Daily Scale Exercises for the Violinist (Chang)
Finger Positions for the Violin (Gilland)
Forty Studies for Violin (Chang)
Past the Print (Waller)
Pluggin In: A Guide to Gear and New Techniques for the 21st Century Violinist (Deninzon)
Practice for Performance for Violin (DeForest)
Progressive Scale Studies for Violin (Bauer)
Sensible Scales Plus! (Waller)
Speed-Reading for Violin (Bauer)
The Violin/Fiddle Manual and Encyclopedia of Techniques:
How to Do Anything on the Instrument (Willis)
Warm-Ups for the Violinist (Wheeler)

WWW.MELBAY.COM

Other Mel Bay Violin Books

100 Christmas Carols and Hymns for Violin and Guitar (C. Duncan)
100 Gospel Songs and Hymns for Violin and Guitar (C. Duncan)
100 Hymns for Violin and Guitar (W. Bay/C. Duncan)
Christmas Melodies for Violin Solo (C. Duncan)
Christmas Solos for Beginning Violin (C. Duncan)
Complete Book of Wedding Music for Flute or Violin (Mickelson)
Gospel Violin (Guest)
Hymn Favorites for Violin (Abell)
Hymn Tunes for Unaccompanied Violin (Carlson)
Hymns for Violin Made Easy (Clarke)
Old English Hymns for Violin Solo (Cummings)
Sacred Hymns for Violin (Isaac)
Sacred Violin Solos (Isaac)
Sacred Melodies for Violin Solo (C. Duncan)
Violin Solos on Early American Hymns Tunes (C. Duncan)
Wedding Music for Solo Violin (Curatolo)
Easy Klezmer Tunes (Phillips)
French Tangos for Violin (Norgaard)
Gypsy Violin (Harbar)
Gypsy Violin Classics (Harbar)
Gypsy Violin Basics (Harbar)
Klezmer Collection: C Instruments (Phillips)
Lover's Waltz: Violin Solo or Duet with Piano Accompaniment (J. Ungar)
Easy Clasics for Violin with Piano Accompaniment (Spitzer)
Easy Solos for Violin (Bluestone)
My Very Best Christmas/Violin (Khanagov)
Solo Pieces for the Beginning Violinist (Duncan)
Solo Pieces for the Intermediate Violinist (Duncan)
Jazz Violin Solos (Abell)
Joe Venuti: Never Before...Never Again
Stephane Grappelli Gypsy Jazz Violin (Kliphuis)
Swingin' Jazz Fiddle Solos (Weinstein)

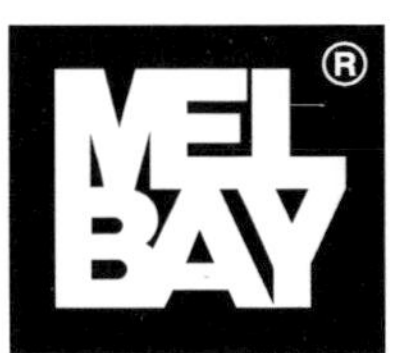

WWW.MELBAY.COM